LOST
BUTLER
COUNTY

LOST
BUTLER
COUNTY

Vanished Towns
of the Cedar Valley

··· LINDA McCANN ···

Charleston   London

THE
History
PRESS

Published by The History Press
Charleston, SC 29403
www.historypress.net

First published 2010

Manufactured in the United States

ISBN 978.1.59629.969.6

Library of Congress Cataloging-in-Publication Data

McCann, Linda.
Lost Butler County : vanished towns of the Cedar Valley / Linda McCann.
p. cm.
Includes bibliographical references and index.
ISBN 978-1-59629-969-6
1. Butler County (Iowa)--History, Local. 2. Cities and towns--Iowa--Butler County--
History. I. Title.
F627.B9M35 2010
977.7'29--dc22
2010017383

CONTENTS

CONTENTS

BUTLER COUNTY'S FORTY LOST LOCATIONS

At least forty towns were formed and then dissolved in Butler County, Iowa, over the years from the late 1800s to the early 1900s. It is easy to realize that the towns began from necessity. The farmers in the area needed supplies within a reasonable proximity. The reason behind the "death" of these towns is simple as well: the path of the railroad. If the railroad line did not go through a town, the town began to die. This book will explore these topics and give some history of the ghost towns surrounding Shell Rock, Iowa.

The author of this book thanks those who willingly contributed material or helped in researching the book. Shirley Miller allowed the use of a paper she researched and wrote in the 1980s. She also had a photo of old Coster that is reprinted. Jim and Linda Gates live in the old Lowell area and have collected information and pictures of that town, which they freely shared. Sherri Willey helped in finding more pictures and by assisting with the research. Claire Munson helped by scanning pictures. The librarians at the Benny Gambaiani Library in Shell Rock and the Clarksville Library aided in finding answers to my questions and willingly reprinted items. Thank you so much Diane, Deb and Kristen. Linda's cousins—Peggy Betsinger Homeister, Mary Phelps Stille and Sandy Adair Soash—proofed and read the information and helped make sure Linda's thoughts were clear and readable. Thanks so much, Peggy, Mary and Sandy! Thanks also to Diane Harms and Sherri Willey for reading and catching things. Dean and Sandy

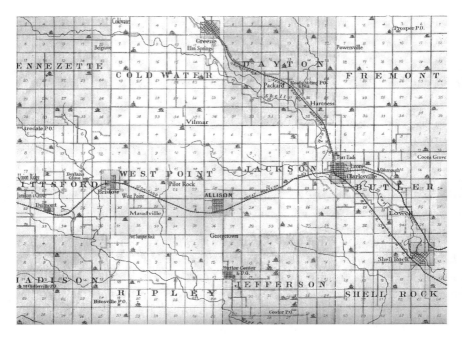

A map of the northern portion of Butler County, showing locations of many of the lost towns. *1906* Butler County Atlas, *printed by the* Times-Republican, *Marshalltown, Iowa.*

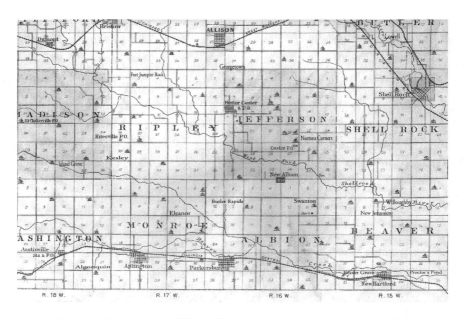

A map of the southern portion of Butler County, showing locations of many of the lost towns. *1906* Butler County Atlas, *printed by the* Times-Republican, *Marshalltown, Iowa.*

Soash had several old plat books I could not have found anywhere else. This is a community-wide project, and thanks are extended to everyone who contributed in any way.

People who contributed to a specific town include:

Butler Center—Linda Cassman Randall

Coster—Shirley Miller

Lowell—Jim and Linda Gates

Norton's Corners—Paul Franken, Fannie Franken Albrecht and Jim Norton

Swanton—Diane Van Mill and Vopal Youngberg

As always, I dedicate the book to my granddaughters, Patricia, Brianna and Danica. Girls, your ancestors did much to make you proud. Lots of love, Grandma Linda.

Every effort has been made for the information contained in this book to be as accurate as possible. The author is not responsible for inaccuracies or disputes.

WHERE DID THEY GO?

Iowa became a state in 1846. Butler County was formed in 1851 from land that was annexed from Black Hawk and Buchanan Counties. The 1852 census shows 73 people living in Butler County. The 1856 census tallies 2,141 inhabitants in Butler County. The 1859 census numbered 6,918 people living in Butler County. Iowa was fashioned as a state of small towns. Small towns, not cities, have shaped the character of Iowa.

Between the two great rivers, small towns sprang up as the prairie soil was turned into farmland. As the counties were formed, towns near the center of the county vied to become the county seat. The goal was that farmers in the farthest corner of the county could get to the courthouse and back home in a day's travel. The county seat usually grew into the largest town in the county. The most important function of the small town was providing goods and services to area farm families.

As pioneers moved west and north from the eastern Iowa towns of Dubuque, Cedar Rapids and Waterloo, the journey to go for supplies became more difficult. To return to Waterloo/Cedar Falls from Butler County took a full day of travel by horseback. Traveling by wagon took longer. Settlers banded together so that several wagons would go for supplies while those left behind oversaw the neighbors' farms. Chores and protecting their families were left to those not going for provisions, and their stores would be purchased and delivered to them.

When the men left to go for goods, they did not know what would happen in the three or more days they were gone. Someone might die, their house or barn might burn down or they might arrive home to find another catastrophe awaiting them. Similarly, a man leaving for supplies might never be heard from again. He might be injured on the road and, having no one to help him, perish from exposure. Either Indians or robbers could attack and kill him. There were instances in which a man did not arrive home when expected and the family never found out what happened to him.

Life was volatile on the prairie. Nothing was taken for granted. Most homesteaders could grow much of their own food but needed to purchase sugar, spices and coffee. They also had to buy farm tools, kitchen utensils, material to make clothes and medicines.

After a few families had settled in the same neighborhood, it was exciting when someone would open a general store. The owner of the general store would now make the journey for provisions; the farmers need only travel a short distance to the store. This made their lives much easier. This partially explains why there were so many little towns within such a small area. Traveling two to three miles was still an event, so each farmer wanted a village within that distance.

Stores were usually the first businesses to open. They tried to stock everything a family needed. Farm wives traded butter and eggs in exchange for credit toward their purchases. When farmers had no money, the general store owner could offer them credit until they sold their crops or livestock. As towns grew, stores came to specialize in particular items like shoes or hardware, but in the early days, the general store carried everything.

The blacksmith shop was another essential service. Horses needed shoes and plow blades needed sharpening. The blacksmith sometimes also operated a livery stable that fed, sheltered and rented out horses.

Other businesses followed. A hotel was important. Most villages soon had one or even two newspapers. Doctors made house calls on sick patients and stayed with mothers delivering babies. Additionally, Iowa law required schools to be located on every other section, so the farthest a student would need to journey to school was two miles. Thus, many towns sprang up near schools. Once a general store and school were in place, most times a mill would soon be built. A mill was important, as farmers needed the mill to grind their crops into flour or other feeds. A nearby sawmill was also needed to cut trees into lumber so the settlers could build houses and barns.

Once a school was built, often church services began in the school. Before long, a church would be built. Ministers provided spiritual guidance and comfort to their congregations. Most small towns had several Christian churches reflecting the diverse religious beliefs of early settlers.

In the 1860s, 1870s and 1880s, Iowa was gripped by a fever for building railroads. Every town wanted to be included on a railroad line. In fact, it was so important to be on a railroad that if the new line did not come to an existing town, towns sometimes "moved" to the railroad, meaning that local residents would actually move their homes and stores a few miles to the rail line. Railroads themselves often created their own towns. In the 1850s, the government gave land to four railroad companies to help them build lines from the Mississippi to the Missouri River.

Butler County is made up of sixteen townships and spread over ninety-six miles. According to the website Iowa's Ghost Towns, at least forty towns had post offices and functioned as small villages during the late 1800s. It is surprising how many villages formed in this small area. Most are no longer functioning, although people in the area still refer to them by name.

ALGONQUIN AND AREDALE

ALGONQUIN

Algonquin was located in Washington Township, Section 25. Algonquin was the name of an Indian tribe located in the region that became Iowa, prior to statehood. Many of the towns in this area have Indian names.

Washington Township was settled in the spring of 1853 by brothers, Elery and Reuben Purcell, in Sections 24 and 25. Elery put up a house, the first in the township. In the spring of 1854, he sold his claim to Roby R. Parriott, a native of Virginia. Parriott went to Illinois to fetch his family, which numbered sixteen people, and returned to his claim in late July 1854. He built a larger home and used it for a hotel, the first and only hotel kept in this township. The first post office in the township was established here in 1855, with R.R. Parriott as postmaster. He used his hotel as the post office.

The hotel became a stage station in 1855, and Parriott erected a large frame home. Many farmers arrived and settled in Washington Township in 1855. There does not seem to have been many businesses in this area. Morris Whitney arrived from New York in 1855. A schoolteacher by profession, he divided his time between teaching and farming. The first school in Washington Township was held in Morris Whitney's home in Section 24 during the summer of 1857. In 1857, a blacksmith shop was located in the township.

In 1865, the post office was moved to Aplington, and Algonquin soon ceased to exist as a town.

AREDALE

Aredale is located in Pittsford Township and is still a collection of houses and a few businesses. In 2001, businesses in Aredale included a bank, tiling company, grocery store, elevator, garage and gospel hall. The city also had a volunteer fire department.

The Aredale name has no historical significance. It is just a nice, fanciful name chosen for the town.

In 1868, a school building for District Number 9 was located on Section 32. In 1873, the building was moved to Section 29. The first school in this district was taught in the house of Sylvanus Hamlin, in 1862, by Mrs. Mary Smith. The schoolhouse in District Number 9 continued to serve the pupils of the town of Aredale. Soon thereafter, the number of pupils became too large to be accommodated in any one building. Temporary quarters were secured for part of the children in a room over the bank, and an additional teacher was hired for these children. There is no longer a schoolhouse in Aredale. The high school students were transferred to Dumont in 1940. The school was finally closed in 1957.

In the spring of 1890, a group of farmers met at Pittsford Number 3 Schoolhouse. They decided a cheese factory would be located on the southwest corner of a farm, one mile south of the present town of Aredale.

In 1900, the construction of the line of the Northwestern Railroad through the western portion of the township led to the establishment of the town of Aredale, an unincorporated village, situated at the center of Sections 29, 30, 31 and 32. Since the railroad was not going directly through the town site, it was decided that Aredale should be moved one mile north. It was laid out and platted by the Iowa and Minnesota Town Site Company. The plat was recorded on June 28, 1900. The town began to grow, lots were sold and business places were soon built. The Aredale Centennial Book states there were two general stores, a hardware store, a drugstore, a bank, an elevator, two lumberyards, a telephone office, a billiard hall and a barbershop.

In 1901, the Evangelical Church of Aredale was organized with six charter members: Mr. and Mrs. August Fassler, Mr. and Mrs. W. Frank Pencook, Louisa Fassler and Henry Fassler. The cost of the new church was $4,158.13. Ruth Diercks's *A Type of Foxfire History from Butler County, Iowa*, states that membership had increased to fifty people by 1905, so a parsonage was built in 1911. The Evangelical Church and the Methodist Church combined in 1968 and continue as the United Methodist Church.

Aredale street scene in 1905. Butler County Centennial Fair Book.

In 1911, the township voted to raise the sum of $5,000, through two annual tax levies, to be used for the construction of a modern schoolhouse for the children of Aredale. According to the *Atlas of Butler County, Iowa*, in 1917, the population of Aredale was fifty-two citizens.

The post office for Aredale was established in 1901 and is still in use. The mail was brought from Dumont twice a week. John Becker was appointed the first postmaster.

For many years, June 28 was observed as Field Day in Aredale. There was a lively celebration. Some of the biggest attractions were the baseball games. Aredale had many good teams, and crowds always overflowed the town.

BEAR GROVE, BEAVER GROVE, BELGROVE, BOYLAN'S GROVE, BUTLER CENTER AND BUTLER RAPIDS

BEAR GROVE

Bear Grove was later named Island Grove. Both towns were situated chiefly in Madison Township, Sections 26 and 27 and portions of 34 and 35 north of Mayne's Creek. This grove originally covered a tract of land about two miles in length from east to west and a mile in width from north to south. The Charles and Margaret Stuart family settled on the side hill, where a large grove of wild plum trees was located. The Stuart children talked about the wild plums and rattlesnakes that surrounded their home all their lives. Two of the Stuart boys were sent one day to bring home the cows. They heard a rustle and noise in the brush and then saw a bear. Luckily, it hurried away from the boys. The area became known as Bear Grove from that incident, according to *A Type of Foxfire History*.

The first post office in the vicinity of what is now New Hartford was established at Beaver Grove in 1855. Silas B. Ensign was appointed postmaster. This office was short-lived because of another settlement, Taylor's Hill, just a half mile away. The government chose to supply the Taylor's Hill office, so Bear Grove Post Office ceased to exist and was renamed New Hartford.

BEAVER GROVE

Beaver Grove was located in Beaver Township, Section 32. Nicholas Hartgraves settled here in 1852. A Beaver Grove Cemetery was located in Section 24. The post office was established in 1855 with S.B. Ensign as the postmaster. The post office was discontinued in 1857 because of the post office at nearby Taylor's Hill, which was another site that served as a post office only; no village was built there, according to the *Butler County Centennial Fair Book.*

BELGROVE

Belgrove, in Bennezette Township, Section 12, was about six miles west of Greene. The post office operated during 1869 only.

BOYLAN'S GROVE

Boylan's Grove was established on Section 24, Pittsford Township. The area was settled by John Boylan and James Matterson Park in the fall of 1852. The men were brothers-in-law and were the first settlers in the eastern part of Pittsford Township. Other brothers—Isaac, James and Asa Boylan— arrived shortly thereafter.

The *1883 Butler-Bremer County, Iowa History* tells how settlers usually made their claims by laying four logs as the foundation of a house and cutting the claimant's name into the timber. Most of the settlements were near a water source. The land had to be cleared of trees in order to farm it. The prairie land would have been easier to clear and farm, but no water was near that area.

The first school in the township was taught during the winter of 1859–60 at the house of Thomas Hewitt by Miss Mary A. Rich, with an attendance of about fifteen scholars. The schoolhouse at that time stood about a mile east of what is now the town of Bristow.

According to Irving Hart's *History of Butler County, Iowa:*

> Up until the winter of 1856–57, buffalo, deer and elk were found in large numbers in Butler County, especially in the western part around what was called Boylan's Grove. So far as meat was concerned, the settlers fared

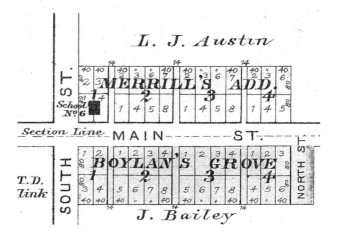

BOYLAN'S GROVE
LOCATED IN PITSFORD TWP.
Scale 300 feet to one Inch.

Boylan's Grove village layout. *1906* Butler County Atlas, *printed by the* Times-Republican, *Marshalltown, Iowa.*

sumptuously every day. In the winter of 1856–57, snow fell in such unusual quantities that it was three feet deep on the level. Alternate thawing and freezing caused ice to form over the top of the snow, which was strong enough to bear the weight of a man, but not sufficiently solid to support the weight of the deer or elk. They would break through the crust and, floundering in the soft mass beneath, become so impeded in their progress as to fall an easy prey to their pursuers, whether hunters, dogs or wolves. As a consequence, nearly all the deer and elk were destroyed that winter. By actual count, at what was known as Jamison's Grove, within the space of two miles up and down the West Fork, thirty-two deer were killed during this season. Many were killed with axes and hatchets without the aid of dog or gun. After that month, few deer and no elk were ever again seen in Butler County.

The first post office in the area was located at Boylan's Grove. The post office existed from 1859 to 1875. In 1862, it was removed to West Point and remained there until 1864, when it returned to the original site. James Butler served as postmaster until 1868, when it was returned to West Point, according to the *1883 Butler-Bremer County, Iowa History.* Henry Early was the first postmaster.

The Boylan Grove Church held a Mission Conference in 1861, made up of the meetings from Hall's Grove, Hitesville, Coldwater, Needhamville and Union Ridge. Later, Ingham and Four Mile Grove were added. During the years 1867–68, membership reached forty-two members. In 1876, the name was changed to Bristow. The first parsonage was built in 1877, one mile east of Bristow. This was later moved into the town of Bristow. The church building was constructed in 1888 and a parsonage in 1916. The parsonage was sold in 1974, when the church no longer had a resident minister. Services continue in the church.

Boylan's Grove was located about one mile west of the current town of Bristow. It was moved to Bristow to be closer to the railroad. Bristow was the center of the railroad division of the Great Western Railroad. It was one of the main stops for fuel, according to *A Type of Foxfire History*.

BUTLER CENTER

The area known as Butler Center is located about eleven miles west of Shell Rock on Butler Center Road, or Blacktop C-45. It was located in the northwest quarter of Section 18 of Jefferson Township.

In the beginning, Butler Center was considered a "point of some importance, being geographically located very near the center of the county," according to the *1883 Butler-Bremer County, Iowa History*. In 1853, Andrew Mullarky of Sturgis Falls (now Cedar Falls) and Colonel James B. Thomas entered the land for Butler Center at the land office in Dubuque. In the spring of 1855, Mullarky and Thomas drew up a plat for the village of Butler Center.

The year 1856 was a progressive and prosperous one. On May 5, Charles Stuart finished building a steam-propelled sawmill for Andrew Mullarky so that the building of a town could begin. Stuart ran the sawmill for four or five years. That same day in 1856, Nathan Olmstead preached his first sermon at the sawmill. The following is related in the *1883 Butler-Bremer County, Iowa History*:

> *Nathan Olmstead came to Iowa in 1853. He was born in Wilton, Connecticut, on the 16th day of September 1809, and is the son of David and Rebecca (Jackson) Olmstead, who were also natives of that State. When Nathan was seven years old, the family immigrated to Tompkins County, New York, where they remained about three years, and then moved to Tioga County, where the son lived until twenty-four years of age. At that time he came west, and after spending one year in LaSalle County, Illinois, moved to what is*

Vanished Towns of the Cedar Valley

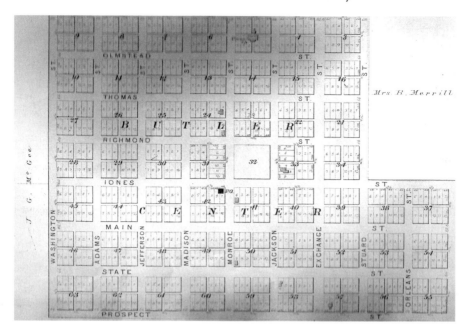

Layout of Butler Center. Butler County Plat Book, *1895. Union Publishing Company, Philadelphia, PA.*

now DeKalb County. In 1842 he joined the Protestant Methodist Church, and soon after, became a minister of the gospel. He followed this calling, as a local preacher, while in that State, and was also ordained a deacon while living there. He settled on Section 18, Beaver Township, Butler County, Iowa in January 1854. In July, 1831, he united in wedlock to Miss Julia Ann Knapp, also a native of Connecticut. Ten children have blessed this union, of whom eight are now living—Melissa, the widow of Henry Tomas; Alonzo, living at Butler Center; Edward, living in Beaver Township; Oscar now living in Waterloo; Orvis, now living in Ackley; Julia Ann, widow of Asa Lee of Ackley; Theodore, living at home; and Lydia, wife of L.H. Boyd.

On May 24, 1856, the Butler Center plat was surveyed and recorded at Clarksville's newly constructed Butler County courthouse. On July 4, 1856, Owen S. Levis opened the first general store in Butler Center. The first school was held in his store and was taught by Alzina Water. Martha Niece later taught school in Enoch George's home and "boarded round." (The name is seen as both Enoch George and George Enoch, and no proof

21

Butler Center general store. *Butler Center, http://www. uni.edu/biology/butlercenter/index.html.*

could be found to what is correct.) It was thought that the children went to the Mullarky School, but Linda Cassman Randall found later that the old creamery had once been the school. In 1883, there was a good school building in Butler Center taught by Misses Ella and Margaret Mullarky. Miss Ella Mullarky was a graduate of the Normal School at Cedar Falls (now the University of Northern Iowa). There were fifty-five students.

Other "firsts" in 1856 included: Joe Santee helped build the very first log home in Butler Center; Dr. H.H. Marsh, dentist, built the third residence; and H.H. Margretz drove stakes to build the first hotel. William Wright was the first blacksmith in Butler Center. The first child born in the village was a son to Martin Bailey in 1856. The first justice of the peace was H.H. Margretz. Herman and Sarah (Stampf) Margretz were natives of Union County, Pennsylvania. They came to Iowa in 1856.

What would a town be without a saloon? The first place of this order was opened during the Civil War by Bennett & Embody. John Court added a billiard hall to the business. The *1883 Butler-Bremer County, Iowa History* reported "there being at times three such places in Butler Center. Under the principle that a town, to build up and secure trade, must furnish the necessary inducement, these places were allowed a free course, and carried on business without molestation. The true sentiment of the people has been recently manifested at the polls. No saloon has been in the village since the removal of the county seat."

Butler Center's first post office was established following the settlement in 1856 to receive "once a week" mail by way of a Cedar Falls carrier. The first postmaster's position was filled by H.H. Margretz, followed by Hugh Mullarky, W.A. Lathrop, J.H. Plater and H.N. Walker. In 1871, daily mail service began with mail coming from Waverly by way of Clarksville. The post office sold its first money order to George M. Craig in July 1875.

The *1883 Butler-Bremer County, Iowa History* reported:

W.A. Lathrop is one of the oldest lawyers practicing in Butler County. He is a native of New London, Connecticut, where he was born in 1826. He is of old Puritan stock, tracing his lineage back to the Rev. John Lathrop, who came over from England, and settled at Scituate, Massachusetts, September 28, 1634. He was admitted to the Bar in 1854 and immigrated to Illinois. He came to Butler County in 1860, settled in Butler Center and resided there in the practice of his profession until the removal of the county seat to Allison, when he took up residence there. Mrs. Lathrop is the former Miss Adelaide Hyde, a native of Connecticut. They have one daughter, Ethel, wife of Mr. Charles W. Levis, the junior member of the firm.

Unfortunately, the summer of 1856 brought with it the need for a township cemetery. Located half a mile east on what is now C-45, it first became the final resting place for four young children. The first recorded deaths that summer were Freddie Santee (August 27), Elizabeth Jane Stuart (August 28), John Stuart (September 3) and Mary Ellen Conn (September 5).

The year 1857 brought Ohioans C.H. Chamberlain, Dr. H.H. Shaw and Enoch P. George to town together to plant their roots in Iowa soil. Chamberlain started a store and built a new house. Shaw was the first practicing physician in town, and he also built a house. George was a carpenter by trade, and he, too, built himself a house in town. All three men stayed only a few years before returning to Ohio.

Two more businessmen took part in the progress of Butler Center that year. Thomas Bird built and stocked a general store with merchandise. Records show that the store was still there in 1883. Franz Digman bought the Santee building and opened a shoe shop, to which he added a general assortment of dry goods and groceries.

The law profession found its way to Butler Center, too. George A. Richmond, the first lawyer in town, bought one-half interest in the town. He built a large residence that was later used as a hotel. After the removal of the town, it was once again used as a residence. After the construction of the courthouse in Butler Center, Orson Rice housed his law practice there. Other businesses were also housed in the courthouse. The *1883 Butler-Bremer County, Iowa History* offers the following description of Rice:

Orson Rice was a native of Ohio, coming to the State from Illinois, arriving in Butler County in 1854, and taking a claim. He was a man of about 28 years of age and had a family. He was very illiterate and knew nothing at all of law when he commenced practice; but he was energetic, independent, and entirely reckless as to the language he used. He would murder the English language and grammar in a way that often made him the laughing

The Butler County Courthouse while it was located in Butler Center. *Butler Center, http://www.uni.edu/biology/butlercenter/index.html.*

stock. He remained in the county, practicing law, until 1884, when he removed to Spirit Lake, and is still at his profession, having served one term as District Attorney, and came very near the Circuit Judgeship.

By 1860, it appears that there was a strong desire to locate the county courthouse in the actual center of the county. A petition was circulated to move it to Butler Center. After several elections, some of which were considered less than ethical, a vote with a majority of eighty caused the courthouse to be relocated in Butler Center. So, beginning in 1860, and for a period of twenty years, Butler Center had the courthouse. It was a small, two-story frame building, twenty-six feet by thirty-six feet, with an outside wooden stairway. It was built at a total cost of about $20,000, which equals $425,000 in 2003 dollars, according to an inflation converter. Andrew Mullarky, a farmer who owned considerable land in that vicinity, donated the two acres on which the courthouse at Butler Center was located. A wooden sidewalk from the courthouse to one of the stores was known to exist even into the 1900s.

In 1865, the population of Butler Center was shown as 390 people, according to the *Iowa State Gazette.*

According to A.T. Andreas in his 1875 *Illustrated Historical Atlas of the State of Iowa*, Butler Center was, except for it being the county seat, "a place of no commercial or other importance." Andreas continues, "The village contains, besides the court house, so called, two general stores, and wagon and blacksmith shops. The best public structure in the place is a two-story frame school house, 20x40, capable of seating 160 pupils." In the years following, people became disenchanted with Butler Center because of its inaccessibility, particularly in the winter.

Reporting all the activity between 1860 and 1861 was William Haddock in Butler Center's first newspaper, the *Butler County Jeffersonian.* An article later that summer in the August 26 issue reported the following: "Notice is hereby given that Rev. Richard Merrill, Presbyterian, will preach at the

Butler Center Church and parsonage

Church and parsonage.

courthouse in Butler Center on Sunday morning September 1 at 11:00 am." After thirty-six issues, Haddock sold the newspaper so he could serve in the Civil War, which had already begun on April 12. In October, Martin Bailey bought the paper and renamed it the *Stars and Stripes*. The *1883 Butler-Bremer County, Iowa History* offers the following information about Bailey:

> *Martin Bailey is a resident of Butler Center, and is one of the editors of the agricultural department of the* Allison Tribune. *He has taken an interest in Butler County since August 1856. At that time, he engaged in general merchandising at New Hartford, and was therefore the first merchant of that place. In 1855, he associated D.N. Root as partner, and the business continued under the firm name of Bailey & Root; but Mr. Bailey soon became convinced he would never be a successful merchant, and in the winter of 1858–9, he purchased his partner's interest and closed out the business. In 1859, Mr. Bailey was appointed deputy county clerk and made out the tax lists for that year. In January, 1860, he became deputy county treasurer, removed to Butler Center, then the county seat, and served in that capacity for over two years. In 1865 he was transferred to Dubuque and afterward to Waterloo, where he was discharged in October 31, 1865. He then returned to his home, and has since been engaged in farming. He now owns a fine herd of Jersey cattle. His farm, continuing 160 acres, lies adjoining the village plat of Butler Center, and his home is supplied with all the necessaries of the best social life. He is a lover of the public schools and always takes an active interest in education. Martin Bailey is the son of Joseph and Patty (Tullar) Bailey. He was born in Oswego County, New York, November 7, 1819. At the age of twenty, he commenced teaching, and taught thirteen winter terms.*

In 1845 he emigrated to Illinois, where in 1847, he married Miss Mary A. Clark, a native of Vermont, and in 1853, came to Iowa and settled in Black Hawk County. In 1854 he was elected clerk of the court and served one year. When the county seat was removed from Cedar Falls to Waterloo, he resigned the office, and became employed in Andrew Mullarky's store for a year. Mr. and Mrs. Bailey have five children—two now living—Cilia and Datus.

The year 1871 brought forth the beginning of daily mail on the Waverly route by way of Shell Rock. Weekly mail was also received from Parkersburg for two or three years, then triweekly and, afterward, daily.

In 1873, the Reverend William Smith organized the Presbyterian Church at Butler Center. The first members were James Barlow and wife, James Hunter and wife, W.C. Thompson and wife, Mrs. B.J. Merrill, Miss Emma Tompkins, James Robbins and wife, Duncan McGregor and wife and Duncan Stewart and wife. Reverend John Gourley succeeded Reverend Smith in 1875. The society had a membership of about twenty-five in 1883, and meetings were held in the former courthouse.

There was an active Sabbath School in the village from about 1864. The first superintendent was George Craig. In the 1880s, there was a membership of forty with an average daily attendance of twenty-five.

The 1875 *Illustrated Historical Atlas of the State of Iowa* shows the following businesses in Butler Center: attorneys at law, titles and abstracts, billiard parlors, carpenters and contractors, two general merchandise stores, hotel, real estate dealer and wagon-maker. Under the patron directory from the same source are listed a stock dealer, mason, stone quarry proprietor and Butler County deputy sheriff. Many of those listed arrived in Butler Center as early as 1840.

This item was found in the *Shell Rock News* of December 15, 1878:

Last Saturday being a beautiful day, we "hooked up" our nag, and took a ride to Butler Center, the county capital. We arrived there about noon and put up at Mr. F. Digman's hotel. It was our first acquaintance with Digman, and we found him to be a very pleasant, courteous and genial gentleman, and always ready to entertain guests. His hotel is new and conveniently arranged, and the table—well that was furnished with everything good and palatable, the hungry could wish for. About the Court House, business was not as flourishing as it has been although the officers appeared to be doing something. We had a pleasant chat with Treasurer Thomas and Auditor Chase. Clerk Burdick was busy, with a number of books, preparing to surrender the office to his successor.

Vanished Towns of the Cedar Valley

By 1878, the railroad ties were laid for the new Dubuque & Dakota Railroad about five miles north of Butler Center. In June 1879, the trains were running. Butler Center was running out of time. The decision to bypass the town led to its disappearance. The *Illustrated Historical Atlas of the State of Iowa* reported:

> *Induced by these considerations, the apparently probable permanency of the county seat, and the flattering prospects for the future, lawyers, doctors, editors, dentists, representatives of the different professions, exponents of various religious creeds, and other necessary elements of civilization, came together and formed a settlement, and it seemed for a time that Butler Center was certainly destined to become the "future great" of Butler County. But now? The deserted streets, empty house, vacant lots, dilapidated fences, signs of dissolution and decay, present themselves on every hand, speaking of things that were, suggesting things that "might have been." This change has been wrought mainly by the relocation of the county seat, the lack of railroads being the main factor which occasioned its removal.*

Soon, the 1880 town presented an appearance of a "place on wheels" as house after house made its disappearance and traveled toward Allison, pulled by Ike Neal's steam engines. About forty houses and stores were moved out of the village. In 1881, Mrs. Franz Digman moved her hotel to Allison, where it became the Allison House. That fall, the Butler County Courthouse was removed to the new town of Allison.

By the year 1883, Butler Center had only one store owner left, Horatio N. Walker. He also acted as the town postmaster. The only blacksmith shop was owned and operated by John McCarty. Sadly, the year 1890 brought the close of the Butler Center Post Office. The *1883 Butler-Bremer County, Iowa History* reported:

> *H.N. Walker, the Postmaster and storekeeper, is an honest, upright gentleman, social with everybody, courteous to all, whose removal would prove a public calamity. He purchased the business of H.C. Plater, in 1871. He has had several different persons associated as partners at different times, until 1878, since which time he has conducted the business alone. He was appointed the Postmaster in 1871. Mr. Walker was born in Vermont, January 17, 1830. His parents, Reuben and Lydia (Miller) Walker, were also natives of said State. He was brought up on a farm in the Green Mountain State, where he remained until 1865, when he came to Iowa and engaged in the dairy business at Dubuque until he came to Butler*

Center. In 1869, he married Miss Caroline French, of Vermont, a native of Pennsylvania. They now have six children—Viola, Lydia, Minnie, Lottie, Abbie and Charles.

The George Martin family moved one of the oldest houses in Allison from Butler Center in September 1879. It is located at 322 Third Street today. Another house that has moved is located on a farm several miles west of the Butler Center site, according to Linda Cassman Randall.

The only building remaining today from the original town is the one that at one time was the Walker Store. The house belongs to the family of the late Casjen Wildeboer. Mr. Wildeboer remembered hearing his parents and grandparents telling about the little village of Butler Center. He told of a drain tile dug up by two of his uncles on both sides of "old Highway 14" from Vilmar through Butler Center (Monroe Street) south to the West Fork of the Red Cedar River. Casjen knew it was there because he dug down to it by the road that goes by the house where he lived and connected his house drain to it. He even found pieces of iron in the field across from his farmyard where the blacksmith once had his shop.

Today, however, we see cornfields and modern farmsteads. The question is, what happened to make all this disappear from the landscape of central Butler County? Butler Center, Iowa, was a pretty spot, located near the center of Butler County about a mile from the West Fork River on a gentle rise overlooking the country for miles around. It became a bustling village consisting of general stores, hotels, churches, a school, blacksmith shops, a post office, a courthouse, a sawmill, saloons and more than forty homes during the twenty-five years (1855–80) of its heyday, according to Linda Cassman Randall.

Even in the 1920s, the *Shell Rock News* was sharing news from the area and calling it Butler Center.

Not far from Butler Center is a huge rock that served as a landmark for early settlers. A story has been retold that this large rock saved the life of Charles Stuart. In the 1860s, Charles set out on foot to see a man several miles away. On his way home, a blizzard blew in and was such that nothing could be seen. Charles tried to keep his bearings, but he was headed directly into the storm, so he staggered as he pushed into the wind. Night was coming on, and Charles feared for his life. Suddenly, a large object loomed in front of him—the rock! He realized he was just a half mile from his home.

The rock was a favorite gathering place for the children in Butler Center. They climbed on its top and slid down the sides. They made up games involving the rock. Besides saving Charles Stuart's life, the rock entertained the children for several generations, according to the *Butler County Centennial Fair Book*.

The old town site of Butler Center, Iowa, is located off Highway 14 between Allison and Parkersburg, Iowa. The old Butler Center Cemetery and Clay Prairie Preserve are a little farther down C-45 toward Shell Rock.

Although the village of Butler Center no longer exists, at least as it once was, residents living in Butler County and around the old town site enjoy keeping the history alive. They have become Butler Center "experts" and enjoy telling its story. They have also organized and refer to themselves as the Friends of Butler Center. The Friends of Butler Center have worked hard to put together a history from the facts and stories that are all that is left of Butler Center. In 1961, a portion of the old Butler Center Cemetery was purchased by the University of Northern Iowa for an outdoor laboratory and as a living example of virgin prairie. Today, these two organizations have teamed together to offer the community educational programs about prairies and Butler Center.

The 2.64-acre virgin tall grass prairie in central Butler County, Iowa, is an unused portion of historic Butler Center Cemetery. Still preserved as a hayfield in 1961, the tract was purchased as a gift to the then State College of Iowa Foundation by Joseph B. Clay, a college alumnus, friend and Cedar Falls native. As one of the University of Northern Iowa's biological preserves, the prairie was dedicated in 1976 as a State of Iowa Preserve to further ensure preservation. The preserve is a small remnant of Iowa's once vast expanse of tall grass prairie, according to the Friends of Butler Center website.

BUTLER RAPIDS

On April 7, 1858, a plat for the town of Butler Rapids was filed with the county judge, A. Converse, and placed in the records. Thomas Maralin entered the first plat and transferred the land to Moses Chapman, or Choplin, of Black Hawk County. The town was to be located on what is now called Jerusalem Hill, which is in Section 7 of Beaver Township, just east of the West Fork River. The land was also known as the "Bolton Place."

At one time, the town contained a store, sawmill and several residences. Most of Butler Rapids' residents moved to Willoughby. In the 1950s, the empty cellar excavations could still be seen. At that time, cottonwood trees, eighteen or twenty inches in diameter, were growing from the cellars, showing that the town had not existed for a number of years, according to *Butler County Cemetery Records*.

CLUTTERVILLE, COLDWATER, COONS GROVE AND COSTER

CLUTTERVILLE

Clutterville was located in southwestern Section 17, Madison Township. A post office served the area from 1890 to 1900. The first postmaster was Alvin B. Watson. Thomas W. Smith was the first teacher in the Clutterville schoolhouse. In 1870, a frame schoolhouse was erected in Section 32. The nearest major town is Dumont.

The 1895 *Atlas of Butler County* shows that Clutterville had a post office, creamery, town hall and school. An abandoned cemetery is all that remains today, according to *Butler County Cemetery Records*.

COLDWATER

Coldwater had a post office for Bennezette Township, Section 6. A post office removed from Franklin County in 1875 to Section 6, Bennezette Township, where it existed until 1885 in the home of John Lockwood. Mail arrived there twice a week from Sheffield and Marble Rock, according to *Butler County Centennial Fair Book*.

The early settlers in the northern part of Butler County have left rather a fragmentary record of a battle between the Winnebago and the Sioux Indian tribes that occurred in the northern part of Bennezette Township. The location of this battlefield is given as in Section 5, about where Coldwater Creek enters the township from the north. The battle seems to have been the concluding one of a campaign that had begun between the tribes sometime previous and somewhere to the north of Butler County. The Winnebago, in retreat, took their stand here and are said to have thrown up earthworks and fortified them as best they could. The Sioux greatly outnumbered their opponents and, attacking them from behind their fortification, brought on a terrific conflict. The Winnebago are reported to have been overwhelmingly defeated. The date of this battle is given as 1853, but this is probably a mistake, as after 1846 there were rarely any large bands of warriors of either of these nations in this territory.

Early settlers in Bennezette Township used to visit the scene of the battle and find there many Indian relics, such as knives, broken guns, arrowheads and Indian jewelry, according to Hart's *History of Butler County, Iowa*.

COONS GROVE

Coons Grove had the first post office in Butler County. It was first settled by Joseph Hicks in December 1850 in Butler Township, Section 13, or about one mile west of the current town of Clarksville. At that time, Hicks's closest neighbor was James Newell, who settled at the forks of the Cedar River, about twenty miles southeast of Hicks.

In the spring of 1851, Henry Hicks, Joseph's father, arrived from Wisconsin and erected a blacksmith's shop. Mrs. Joseph Hicks is considered a true western heroine and is described as able to "talk injine" or shoot a rifle equal to "any other man." The town of Clarksville was laid out and platted in 1853, and most arriving pioneers settled in this area.

In the beginning, mail was brought from Janesville once weekly. With two rivers to cross and no bridges or roads to do so, the post office soon was moved to Leoni.

Joseph Hicks and his family went to Kansas in 1867, and Coons Grove became just a tidbit of history, according to the *1883 Butler-Bremer County, Iowa History*.

COSTER

When viewing the completely rural area that is Coster in 2008, there is very little evidence of the flourishing village that existed in the late 1800s and early

1900s. Coster was located near 25719 Quail Avenue—today the farmstead of Jim and Shirley Miller. From Shell Rock, go west on the Butler Center Road (C-45) seven miles. Turn south on Quail Avenue and go about two miles. Coster was within six miles of the town of Butler Center; proximity was a common occurrence in those days.

Newcomers to the area in 1883 probably found it difficult to believe the description sketched by Van E. Butler, the newspaperman, when he stated, "Twenty years ago the major portion of Jefferson Township was a splendid specimen of Iowa sloughs. Then a man would hardly have dared to cross it without first making his last will and testament and bidding a kind adieu to his family," as recorded in the *1883 Bremer-Butler County, Iowa History*. This would have been the countryside John Coster saw when he moved to Jefferson Township in 1869.

John Coster, for whom the settlement of Coster was named, was born in Mecklenberg-Schwerin, Germany, in 1847, the son of John and Louise (Grove) Coster. In 1860, the family immigrated to McHenry County, Illinois, and John married Minnie Stamer in 1867. John, Minnie and their oldest child arrived in Butler County, Iowa, with $8, three horses and two cows, according to the *Butler County Centennial Fair Book*. John began purchasing land in this area as soon as he could afford to buy it. His first purchase was in 1871 from Henry Yarcho for $1,380, about $17 per acre! He eventually owned four hundred acres for an average price of $33.20 per acre. John worked hard to improve his holdings, including this tract of land. He raised Duroc-Jersey hogs and won many prizes at local fairs. He was president of the Butler County Fair Association from 1904 to 1920 and was given a lifetime membership in the Honorary Presidents Society, according to the *Butler County Centennial Fair Book*.

Early establishments in Coster were a general store, a creamery, two churches, a school and a post office. Church services were held in homes as early as 1866, but it wasn't until 1871 that land was purchased to build the Salem Evangelical Association, later known as the German Evangelical Church, according to Shirley Miller's interview. The German Evangelical Church became the Dutch Reformed Church, which later was destroyed by fire. The land where it once stood is now (2008) owned by Jesse DeGroote. In 1894, some members of the German Evangelical Church became discouraged and dissatisfied and decided to start their own church. This was the start of the United Evangelical (Methodist) Church. It closed in 1928 and was dismantled in 1939. Letrisha Wise owned this land in 1984.

Mr. and Mrs. John Coster.
Shell Rock News.

Also on this site was a creamery operated by Isaac Hall. He also conducted a store from his residence. Otis F. Courbat purchased the creamery in 1906, ran it for two years and then dismantled it. He then built a new creamery a half mile north on five acres of land purchased from John Coster. This was across the road from Salem Cemetery, which later became known as Coster Cemetery. The cement blocks used to build the creamery were made at the site. Butter made at the creamery was hauled to the depot in Shell Rock and then shipped to the New York market. A group of local farmers formed a cooperative and bought the creamery in 1917. It was closed in 1925. The 1917 population of Coster stood at sixteen people, according to the *Atlas of Butler County, Iowa.*

Five years after Mr. Courbat built the creamery, he constructed a general store. His brother-in-law, Will Craner from New York State, moved to Coster and managed the store until 1917, when Newton Ramige bought it. All of the merchandise in the store was hauled in by a team of horses and a wagon from the Shell Rock depot nine miles away, according to the Courbat interview. The store became a weekly meeting place for the farmers in the area. They purchased their groceries, visited and played cards on Saturday nights. The wives visited at the home of the storekeeper or the butter maker's

The Otis Courbat Creamery at Coster before the store was built. Butler County Centennial Fair Book.

house while the children played games like skip to my Lou or musical chairs. Mildred (Hartwig) Mohn remembered her family taking eggs to the store to trade for groceries or dry goods. There were big bunches of bananas hanging on a stick, huge barrels of pickles, flour and sugar in one-hundred-pound sacks and large boxes of cookies with hinged glass lids. The only food in cans was pork and beans and a few kinds of fruits. Claus Harms, John Modderman, a Mr. Shanks from Waterloo and August Yarcho all owned the store for periods of time before it closed in the early 1940s.

An icehouse, storage building for supplies and barn for eight horses were also built in Coster by O.F. Courbat. During the winter, the creamery patrons came and helped "put up," or store, ice from the West Fork River. The following summer, they could come to the icehouse and get free ice to make ice cream. One winter, Mr. Courbat and his nephew, Ernest, were busily removing snow from the ice on the river, working with a team of horses pulling a drag. Suddenly, a big chunk of ice broke off, and the horses fell into the icy water. Ernest ran three-fourths of a mile to get help while O.F. held the horses' heads above water. Help finally arrived with a log chain and a team of horses. The chain was placed around the horses' necks, and one by one they were dragged out of the water. However, the older horse was too cold and exhausted to stand up. Not wanting her to freeze to death, the men whipped her until she finally stood up. Neither horses nor men suffered any ill effects.

At one time, there was a blacksmith shop operated by John Baker, according to the Courbat interview. Business was good because people from the surrounding area traveled to Coster with horse and buggy or a bobsled lined with straw for warmth in the winter. They wrapped themselves in horsehair blankets and used heated soapstones or bricks for foot warmers. Many times, fields were used for roadways when snowdrifts closed the roads.

In his teen years, before there was mail service, John Hartwig would walk to Butler Center to pick up the mail. It was then distributed from his parents' home, according to the Mohn interview. A post office was established in 1890, with Isaac Hall serving as postmaster. This office was discontinued in 1902 when rural routes became established. In the wintertime, Mr. Hall put a little homemade structure on his delivery sled. It had a small wood-burning stove inside to keep him warm. A tiny square hole was cut in front where the reins could pass through.

A small grove of trees with a grassed area made a nice park in Coster. Neighborhood picnics were held here, and many programs were presented by the schoolchildren. The men of the community built a stage for the performances. Memorial Day was one of the very special holidays celebrated with a picnic, program and decorating of the graves. Jefferson School No. 2, also known as the Hartwig School, functioned from about the mid-1860s until it closed in 1947 due to lack of teachers, according to the *Butler County Centennial Fair Book*.

The creamery closed in 1925, and the general store closed in about 1940–42. Time brought many changes, and by the early 1940s, the village of Coster was totally dismantled. In 2008, Jefferson Township was once again completely rural. All that remains to prove that Coster ever existed are a couple of crumbling foundations, Coster Cemetery and a few recorded memories. (Researched and written by Shirley Miller. Used with her permission.)

The following is the obituary of John Coster, originally printed in the *Shell Rock News* on August 24, 1924:

> *John Coster, pioneer resident, former active businessman, and well to do land owner, residing at Coster died suddenly at 1 o'clock Tuesday morning. He had been indisposed only since last Thursday and his death was unexpected.*
>
> *He had retired at 8 o'clock in the evening and had felt as well seemingly as he had during the previous four days. The first indication that everything was not well with him was when he was heard to fall to the floor. He had got up during the night and it was then that death struck its final blow. When his room was entered upstairs, he was found lying prostrate on the floor, life being almost extinct.*
>
> *For many years, Mr. Coster was deeply interested and involved in the Butler County Fair Association, serving that organization as its president*

The village of Coster, Iowa, year unknown. *Collection of Shirley Miller, used with her permission.*

for sixteen years. He retired from these labors three years ago when his health gave way. He suffered a paralytic stroke from which he did not recover for many months.

Mr. Coster was the soul of honor and integrity and no man stood higher in Butler County's affections than he. He was active in church and Sunday school work and the community of which he had been practicality its active head for nearly a half century will deeply feel his loss.

Mr. Coster was a well informed man [something about newspapers]. *He always thought it was worthy of encouragement and his death removes one of* THE NEWS *most faithful subscribers.*

He was a man of humane heart and his love of children was as ardent in his old age as when it was fired by the love of his own children in their childhood. He was never too busy to be kind and thoughtful of others' welfare. His stalwart form will no longer be a welcome sight on the streets of Shell Rock. What enemies he had he could well have afforded to be proud of had his humble spirit been so disposed.

He was for years superintendent of the Sunday School. John Coster leaves three children to mourn his loss—John of Muscatine, Henry S. of Shell Rock, and Mrs. N.S. Ramige of Coster.

The funeral rites will be held in the church at Coster tomorrow (Friday) afternoon at 2:30.

ELEANOR AND ELM SPRINGS

ELEANOR

Eleanor was located in Monroe Township, Section 15. It was a hamlet and railroad station formerly on the Chicago & North Western Railroad in the central part of Monroe Township. The train depot served passengers, and the stockyards were used by farmers for marketing their cattle and pigs. The town was surveyed and platted in May 1900.

The town was named for Mrs. Eleanor McDonald. The post office was named Oplington. Both Eleanor and Oplington were located close to present-day Aplington. The post office was established in 1901, with Joseph Nicklaus as first postmaster. It was discontinued in 1903. The town consisted of a general store, an elevator, a farm machinery sales company, a school and several houses. The 1917 population in Eleanor is listed as sixteen, according to the 1917 *Atlas of Butler County, Iowa*. The store closed in the 1920s.

ELM SPRINGS

Elm Springs was located in Coldwater Township, Section 12. A village plat was laid out, surveyed and recorded just south of the current town of Greene. John Miller secured the land in 1854 and built a small cabin near a group of springs that gushed from the base of elm trees. The cabin was opened for travelers and was the first hotel in the Greene area. A post office was attained by these early pioneers in 1855 and named Elm Springs. John

Miller was postmaster, and his home was his office.

Jesse Ohmert was appointed postmaster in 1870, and the post office moved to his home. The post office was changed to Greene in 1871 and moved into the area where the businesses were growing and the town expanding, according to the 1883 *Butler-Bremer County, Iowa History*.

Miller's cabin was used as a stagecoach stop in the early days, as it was on the route between Cedar Falls and Mason City. Elm Springs did prosper until a railroad was extended to the area one mile north of the town. Then, the name was changed to Greene, and Elm Springs ceased to exist. The cabin was moved to the Butler County Fair Grounds in Allison in 1956. It was taken apart and the logs moved to the fairgrounds, where it was reassembled on a new concrete floor and foundation. It is open to the public and tours are given, according to the *Butler County Cemetery Records*.

FORT EADS AND
FORT SUMTER ROCK

FORT EADS

Fort Eads was an area near Clarksville. January 1854 marked the beginning of the troubles between the Iowa settlers and the Sioux Indians, a conflict which eventually culminated in the Spirit Lake massacre. The fort's mere existence is indicative of the fact that the possibility of an invasion by hostile Indians was ever-present in the minds of these early settlers.

Fort Eads was used one time only, and W.L. Pahnei, in a "History of Clarksville" in the *1883 Butler-Bremer County, Iowa History*, gives a graphic description of the Indian scare of 1854 in Butler County.

> *In the spring or early part of the summer of 1854, the nerves of the white population of North-central Iowa were set into a terrible flutter by the announcement that the noble "red men" were greatly incensed by the appearance of numerous pale faces within their, to them, legitimate territory, and that they proposed to massacre, at one fell swoop, every man, woman and child. Had the shock of an earthquake or the coming of a second deluge been announced, with as much probable certainty, the panic could not have been more successful, and for days and nights, the most timid might have been seen rapidly running toward the south. In some instances everything was left in the rear except sufficient to sustain life until a "heavier settlement" could be reached. But all did not act thus. The bugle*

was sounded, the standard unfurled, and courageous volunteers rallied to its support.

Colonel Abner Eads, at that time superintendent of public instruction for the state, happened to be in Cedar Falls. Having been an officer in the army, during the war with Mexico, he was immediately elected impromptu commander-in-chief of all the forces that were about to engage in the prolonged and bloody campaign, and promptly set himself about organizing, drilling and reviewing two companies of volunteer "dragoons." During the re-organization, M.M. Trumbull, who was a sergeant of artillery in the Mexican war, and had distinguished himself in the battles of Palo Alto, Monterey, Chapultepec, etc., was honored by the Colonel with the position of adjutant-general and chief-of-staff.

Edward Brown was captain of the company from Black Hawk and Jerry Farris of that from Bremer. So as soon as the roads and weather would permit, "Brigadier" Eads headed his noble column and boldly struck out for the frontier. When the column had reached Clarksville, its ranks were considerably swollen by the gradual "falling-in" of strong-hearted recruits from the wayside.

At Clarksville, it halted for supper, a night's rest and a council of war, after a forced march of twenty-five miles. The refreshments were generously furnished by the remaining citizens who were so extremely patriotic that they would not "take a cent"; but when the troops proceeded the next day, found they had been eaten out of "house and home." The decision at the council of war no man knew, save those in authority, but were compelled to "guess" from the proceedings which followed. A small detachment of "regulars" was left with the citizens, under orders to erect a fort—on the hill where Mr. Baughman's residence now is—and not delay a moment until its completion. The noble little garrison went manfully to work detailed two-thirds of their number for picket duty, while the rest began sinking trenches and throwing up breast works, never stopping a moment except to eat, drink and sleep. During the progress of this work, the main column had proceeded as far northwest as Clear Lake, and frightened a few whites and a number of Winnebago's almost out of their wits, who thought them red-skins. All the excitement was caused by the murder of a "skinaway" and the scalping of an old "squaw" belonging to the Winnebago tribe, by a marauding band of Sioux. The troops bivouacked for the night, and many were the disappointed heroes who would be compelled to return the next day bearing the sad tale to their friends that the Indian war was a myth, and that they were not permitted, by kind Providence, to wholly exterminate the very name of "Injun" from the face of the earth, by pouring out their life's blood in defense of their homes and firesides. During the home march of the veterans they were not so careful of their powder as on their northern trip, and occasionally amused themselves by discharging a shot at some wayside object, the reports of which "panicked" the remaining settlers, who flew to the protection of Fort Eads, at Clarksville.

Adjutant-General and Chief-of-Staff Trumbull, when the troops went into camp for the night, strolled away in search of the Shell Rock River for the purpose of bathing. While enjoying the refreshing bath, he chanced to observe a woman, near the bank opposite, washing clothes. An idea struck him. He would rush wildly into camp and report that Indians, thousands of them, were on the opposite side of the river and were preparing an attack. The disclosure had the desired effect. "Boots and saddles" was immediately sounded and the bold soldiers were off in a trice; not toward the enemy, but each upon his own hook, bound to receive shelter behind the protecting walls of the little fortification. When the headlong retreat of the troops, who had all been "cut to pieces," was known at the fort by the arrival of the better mounted dragoons—the only ones who escaped with their "har" [hair]— the scenes in the fort could not have been better imagined than described; for there were assembled the women and children! Brave hearts almost ceased to perform their proper functions! Timid women wrung their hands and fainted, while the children wept at beholding the fearful carnage! Quietude was at length restored; a hearty laugh indulged in; the war ended, and all returned to their peaceful homes. Thus closed the Indian massacre of 1854.

The fort was located two blocks west of the present Main Street, on what is now Superior Street. The fort got as far as having a foundation and a couple of logs laid up. A bronze plaque was set in a huge boulder and dedicated on Memorial Day 1929 by the Clarksville American Legion Post No. 452, according to Priepke's *Years Ago*. It reads, "This Hill Marks the Site of Fort Eads—1854."

FORT SUMTER ROCK

Fort Sumter Rock was located in West Point Township on a wagon trail leading from Cedar Falls to the west. It is north of Kesley and about a mile south of Highway 3. It is now on Highway 14, south of Allison.

Fort Sumter Rock is located upon a hill and visible from the surrounding area. It was first painted after the Civil War and continues to the present day. Butler County Centennial Fair Book.

In 1865, everything from Butler County had to go to market in Cedar Falls, and all supplies had to be brought to Butler County from that same area. The railroad only ran as far as Cedar Falls at that time. A man returning from Cedar Falls had news he wished to share but no way to do it. Seeing a large rock on the Lewis Kilson farm, he decided to write on the rock and used axle grease to share his news—the taking of Fort Sumter by Union troops. Shortly thereafter, Lewis Kilson and his son Frank rode past the rock on their way to Bear Grove. They saw the news and spread it to whomever they saw. Frank Kilson kept the rock painted and placed an American flag upon it during his life, according to *A Type of Foxfire History*.

This is another site that is used as a landmark while giving directions, but new residents to the area may have no idea where it is located and why it is named this.

GEORGETOWN, HARTNESS AND HITESVILLE

GEORGETOWN

Georgetown was located at the junction of four townships—West Point, Jackson, Ripley and Jefferson. It was platted and recorded in 1857, embracing forty acres in the exact geographical center of the county. This paper town was called Georgetown, and on paper it made the best appearance of any town in the county. The plat was exceptionally well drawn and the location unquestionably favorable, but the prospective county capital had not a building or a sign of habitation. It existed solely in the imagination of its projectors.

A petition to bring the question of relocation of the county seat at Georgetown was drawn up and extensively signed. This petition was presented to Judge Alonzo Converse, who granted the request and ordered the question submitted to the voters of the county at the April election in 1858. After an active campaign, the matter was decided in favor of leaving the county seat at Clarksville by the narrow majority of 327 to 320. As all the hopes for the future Georgetown had rested upon the successful termination of this campaign, its prospects received a deathblow by this result. No further effort was made to establish a town on this location. It remains, therefore, merely a geographical expression.

Alternately, the Butler County genealogy website contends that on April 5, 1858, twelve votes were cast to remove the county seat from Clarksville to Georgetown, all in favor. Before anything could be done, another election voted to remove it to Allison, and that was done, ending the future of Georgetown.

HARTNESS

Hartness was in Dayton Township, Section 26. The post office was in business from December 4, 1886, to January 5, 1887, with Mrs. Rena Root as postmaster. Mrs. Root later became postmaster at Root's Siding, according to the *Butler County Cemetery Records*.

HITESVILLE

Hitesville was located in Ripley Township, Section 19. The area got its name after J.C. Hites, whose family laid claim to the land in 1855. This was wholly a farming community and had no town or village, no railroad and only a post office. This town was located about three miles northeast of Kesley.

Hitesville Gospel Chapel is still in use in 2010 and draws hundreds of people for meetings twice yearly. Butler County Centennial Fair Book.

The Hitesville Post Office was established in 1871 from the home of J.S. Margretz, the first postmaster. It was on the direct mail route from Aplington to Bristow. The post office closed in 1900, moving to the town of Kesley.

The first school in Ripley Township was held in Section 20 by Miss Susanna Kimmel, in 1858. The building was built expressly to serve as the school, according to the *1883 Butler-Bremer County, Iowa History*.

The United Brethren group constructed a church building here in 1891. The first pastor was Reverend George Trindle. The church continues to be used as the Hitesville Gospel Hall, a nondenominational church. In 1947, the original auditorium was enlarged, and at present, can seat four hundred people on the main floor. An annual Bible Conference is held in September of each year, drawing about six hundred people from various locations, according to the *Butler County Centennial Fair Book*.

In October 1855, the first burial took place in Ripley Township. The Hitesville Cemetery is located in Section 29 of Ripley Township. Hitesville Cemetery is a township cemetery for the use of the surrounding territory. It is tax supported and under the direction of three trustees. It has never belonged to any church, according to usgenarchives.net.

Ingham, Island Grove and Jamison's Grove

Ingham

Ingham was located on maps, but nothing further could be found about it. It had a post office at one time, according to the website www.lat-long.com/ListLocations-1476-Iowa-Post_Office.html.

Island Grove

Island Grove was a post office location in Madison Township, Section 35. Dr. George Sprague was the postmaster and operated his office from his home, which was located on the route from Cedar Falls to Hampton. The post office operated from 1858 to 1868. Island Grove was called Bear Grove in later years.

The Island Grove school, which stands almost exactly in the middle of Section 32 at the southern edge of Island Grove, is rural school district Madison Number 9.

Jamison's Grove

Jamison's Grove was west of Bristow, with a grove of timber nearby. This is an example of how the early settlers used nature to name their locations.

This grove was situated in Sections 19 and 20. Being satisfied with the location and the quality of the land, which he found, Mr. Jamison selected 320 acres. On August 11, 1853, Mr. Jamison made entry of this half section of land in the land office at Des Moines, Iowa, thus making the first original entry of land in the township.

J.R. Jamison was one of the pioneer residents of the county and a member of the bar. He did not maintain an office in any town of the county but had his home on his farm at Jamison's Grove.

In 1868, a general store was established by J.H. Playter at Jamison's Grove, in Section 20. Mr. Harlan resigned the postmastership and secured the appointment of Mr. Playter, who held the office until about 1870. Ross Jamison was then appointed postmaster and held the position until April 28, 1875, when he was succeeded by W.R. Jamison, who served his second term as postmaster until sometime in 1877, when he resigned in favor of James Harlan. There were other aspirants for the office, however, and A.L. Bickford was appointed postmaster and removed the post office to the town of Dumont, about four miles to the southeast of Union Ridge.

The Winnebago annually made a journey through the western part of the county on their way from Clear Lake, in Cerro Gordo County, to a camping ground in the vicinity of James Newell's on the Cedar. Their route led them through Jamison's and Boylan's Groves, thence down the West Fork to its junction with the Cedar.

Presbyterians at one time had a strong organization at this place. The church was established at Jamison's Grove on October 31, 1857, taking the name of Pisgah Church, according to Hart's *History of Butler County, Iowa*.

KESLEY, LEONI AND LOWELL

KESLEY

Kesley is the only village within the limits of Madison Township. In the 1850s, a stock company was formed in Ohio, known as the Ohio Stock Breeding Association. The members of the association were John K. Green, of Cincinnati; R.W. Musgrave and Luther A. Hall, of Tiffin City; Dr. Sprague and others. Through Dr. Sprague, the originator of the plan, the company purchased some six thousand acres of land, mostly in Madison and Ripley Townships. Dr. Sprague was made the manager of the farm and came to Butler County about 1858, bringing a splendid herd of shorthorn cattle with him. He located in Section 35, in Madison Township, and commenced the construction of buildings for the accommodation of the stock and a house for the men connected with the enterprise. After several years, Dr. Sprague gave up the struggle, the company was dissolved and the land was divided among the stockholders.

Kesley S. Green, son of John K. Green, came to Madison Township in 1865 to take charge of his father's land there. The village of Kesley was platted on his land and is named for him.

The Monroe Reformed Church was organized on June 14, 1885, with a membership of thirty-four families and built a neat church building, which is still used by this organization. This church is located three miles south and a half mile east of Kesley.

In 1900, the line of the Northwestern Railroad was projected through this section of the county. A plat of land was secured by the Iowa & Minnesota

Town Site Company, upon which a town was platted and named Kesley for Mr. Green. The plat of the town of Kesley was filed for record on June 15, 1900, by A.V.E. Brice, representing the Iowa & Minnesota Town Site Company. This railroad was later sold to the Chicago & Northwestern Railway Company.

Before the town was organized, a post office had been maintained for a number of years at Hitesville, several miles to the east. After the town of Kesley came into being, this office was discontinued, and a post office was established at Kesley. The postmasters here have been as follows: John Bode, Henry DeVries and John Wessels. Kesley still has a post office as of 2010.

Soon after the platting of the town, an auction was held by the Town Site Company, at which a sale of lots in Kesley was made. The opening of a lumberyard by Reints & DeBuhr, which later organized the Bank of Kesley, marked the beginning of the actual transaction of business in Kesley. Bode Brothers of Austinville and F. Traisman of Aplington immediately opened general stores, and the Northern Grain Company and the Nye-Schneider-Powler Company built elevators along the right of way. H.E. Perry of Swanton opened a blacksmith shop, Bode Brothers of Parkersburg a drugstore and Lindeman and DeVries a hardware and furniture store. J.H. Brandenburg built a two-story brick hotel, which he operated for some time. A creamery had been in operation about a half mile north of the site of Kesley for some time prior to its founding.

In 1914, Kesley had about 120 inhabitants, two general stores, a drugstore, a hardware and furniture store, an implement establishment, a lumberyard, a bank, two elevators, a meat market, a hotel, a barbershop and pool hall, a harness shop, a milk depot and two blacksmith shops.

An independent school district was formed by Kesley. In 1914, there were two departments in the school, with an attendance of about forty children. The school building is a substantial two-story frame structure, according to Hart's *History of Butler County, Iowa*. In 1917, the population stood at fifty-two, according to the 1917 *Atlas of Butler County, Iowa*.

LEONI

Leoni had a post office located in Butler Township, Section 18. The post office began in Coons Grove in 1853, with Abner C. Clark as the postmaster. It moved to another location in 1855 and was renamed Leoni, with Mr. Clark still serving as postmaster. In 1861, the town was renamed Clarksville, and Charles A. Bannon was postmaster. It was listed in the *U.S. Official Register* as a post office in Butler County from 1855 to 1861 but was not found on the maps, according to the *Annals of Iowa*.

LOWELL

The village of Lowell (or Lowtown, as the locals called it) was located three miles west of Shell Rock. The current address is 30461 205th Street, Shell Rock, and it is the current site of the home of Jim and Linda Gates. The town also included the field to the east of the Gates property. None of the original buildings exist today; only a few foundations and depressions where basements once were can be seen.

Asa Lowe originally bought the land from the United States of America on June 16, 1854, and the town was platted on September 15, 1857. Asa Low(e) (both spellings are used in various locations) came from Vermont and spent some time in Illinois before coming to Iowa in 1854. He is listed in the 1856 census as a lawyer, and the 1875 census lists him as a farmer. One other location listed him as a millwright. This was common on the frontier, as occupations changed to suit the time and the territory. He was married to Amelia and had two living children, Wallace and Emma. The Lowell cemetery records list a stone with "Children" of Asa Lowe on it with no names or dates. These probably were other children who either died before or shortly after birth, which was not uncommon at the time.

Records show that there were two mills in Lowtown, perhaps built by Asa Lowe but operated by S.D. Goughnour. The mills were built very near a rock bottom ford that was once used by the early settlers in the crossing of the Shell Rock River before bridges were built. In the 1875 plat of Butler County, this ford is shown as an extension of 205th Street to the east across the river. These mills were lost on Monday, March 30, 1875, when a huge ice floe on the Shell Rock River destroyed them. The April 1, 1875 article in the *Clarksville Star* relays the account of the loss. There was a huge ice floe on the river due to the spring thaw and rains. The article says that an ice jam threatened the Iowa Pacific Railroad bridge in Clarksville. After a lot of chopping, the ice jam was reduced, and the floe went downstream with no damage to the bridge. A second jam, which was larger than the first, formed shortly after. They worked on the ice by blasting and chopping, and at 2:00 p.m., it dislodged and headed downstream toward Lowtown. At Lowtown there were two mills, a sawmill and the Lowell Flouring Mill. The sawmill stood just below the gristmill. The gristmill fell and set upon the sawmill. "Every effort was

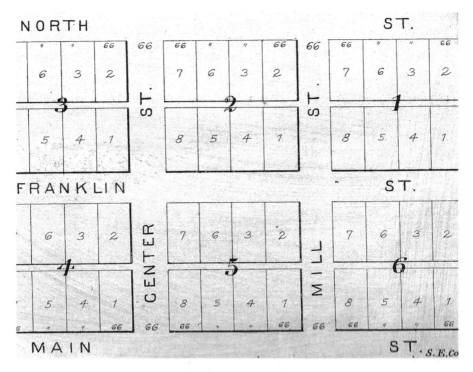

Lowell village layout. *1906 plat book, printed by the* Times-Republican, *Marshalltown, Iowa.*

made to save the mill, but at 3 pm on Monday the whole structure gave away and fell in a complete wreck into the rapid current." The article ends by saying, "As far as we are informed no damage was done at Shell Rock." This was effectively the end of Lowtown.

The only other merchant of Lowtown we can locate was a blacksmith by the name of William Flood. William Flood is buried in the Lowell cemetery as a veteran of the Civil War. The original abstract shows the town lots being sold to about a dozen people, but whether they ever built upon or opened a store there we do not know.

Jim and Linda Gates, Lowell town historians, relate:

> *We have a picture from the Butler County Atlas of the old Lowtown Hotel. The stories we hear are that of an old hotel or stagecoach stop that stood behind our house. It was supposedly used as stagecoach stops and had a metal cell in the basement for housing prisoners. We have no idea when it was built or by whom. It could have been Asa Lowe's original house. We know through the*

Lowell town millstone, 1857. The millstone is located in a stone fence in the town of Clarksville. *Taken by Jim Gates, 2008, used with his permission.*

Lowell Hotel. A Type of Foxfire History from Butler County, Iowa, *1976.*

plat maps that this hotel was at the same site that was listed as his dwelling. Several other foundations can be located, but no information exists about them.

The Lowell School is listed on the 1895 plat map as being at the corner of Vail and 212th Streets. This would currently be the northeast corner of the Shell Rock Ethanol plant property, formerly owned by Eldon Renning.

The author's grandmother, Ethel Harris Phelps, was born in this area, and her birth certificate states place of birth as Lowtown. Ethel Harris was born in January 1900, so the area was still thought of as a town at that time.

Maudville and Monmouth

Maudville

Maudville was located in West Point Township, Section 28, about a mile and a half from the present town of Allison. It was named in honor of Maude Babbage, daughter of B.A. Babbage, who had established the Iowa Central Stock Farm, which was located in the town. This was about 1870. The post office was located here only during 1873.

The Iowa Central Stock Farm comprised more than two thousand acres of land and was one of the best-known farms in the state of Iowa. Babbage, who lived in Dubuque, sent Charles Thompson to manage it. When Babbage failed in business, the farm fell into the hands of H.L. Stout of Dubuque. Stout secured I.M. Fisher as manager of the farm, and he remained there from 1875 to 1891, when Stout purchased the land where the farm buildings stood. While Stout owned the farm, it was known as the "Lexington of the Northwest" because it was famous for developing trotting horses.

The farm was also famous for its deer park, which consisted of artificial woodland where a herd of wild deer were kept. Many people traveled here to picnic and watch the deer. The deer were later sold to a businessman from New York, who transported them to his game preserve in Vermont.

The village had a post office, a blacksmith shop, a rooming house on each side of the road and a newspaper, the *Butler County Times*. C.G. Bundy bought the paper from Parkersburg and moved it in 1872. It ceased publication in 1872.

There was a Maudville schoolhouse located in Section 26 of West Point Township. This school is significant because it was where Carrie Lane taught from December 2, 1878, to March 20, 1879. She had sixteen pupils and boarded with Mr. and Mrs. I.M. Fisher, who lived at the stock farm. Carrie Lane became famous later as Carrie Lane Chapman Catt, one of the national figures in women's suffrage. The Maudville schoolhouse was moved to Allison and used by the Episcopal Church in about 1884. About 1890, John W. Ray bought the building and moved it to his farm in Jackson Township.

At the time of its founding, Maudville showed great promise of developing, but Mr. Babbage lost his company and moved on, and the town soon followed. Most of the buildings and people relocated to Allison, according to the *Butler County Centennial Fair Book.*

MONMOUTH

Monmouth was located in Section 17, Butler Township, about one mile east of Clarksville, as shown on maps of 1869. No record exists of a post office located here.

New Albany, New Albion, New Jerusalem and Norton's Corners

New Albany

New Albany was shown as a town in the book *Place Names Connected with the Chicago and Northwestern Railroad*. It was located in Butler County but just shown as a stop on the railroad. No other information concerning New Albany could be found.

New Albion

New Albion was located about twelve miles west and south of Shell Rock. From Shell Rock, take Butler Center Road (or C-45) eight miles west to the Sinclair Blacktop, or CR-T47. Turn south and go about four miles to New Albion.

The small settlement of New Albion once was located southeast of the cemetery, which is located in Section 33 of Jefferson Township. It was platted about 1856 in Section 3 and 4 of Albion Township. It was quite a flourishing village at one time, having a sawmill, a store and the early Swanton Post Office. The post office was established in 1857 with the name of Swanton, and Jacob Brown was the first postmaster. The post office continued until rural mail delivery began in the county.

The *1883 Butler-Bremer County, Iowa History* included the following reference to New Albion/Swanton:

Marcia A. Hovey is the widow of Lewis Hovey. Her maiden name was Marcia Nefford, and she was born in Glover, Orleans County, Vermont. She married Mr. Hovey in Linn County, Iowa in 1855. They came to Butler County in 1866 and settled first in Swanton. Mr. Hovey died suddenly in April 1877, and Mrs. Hovey continues to live on the homestead farm. She has two children—Julia I and Emma P. The homestead is about 300 acres.

John Bicknell taught school in a log schoolhouse during the winter of 1855–56. It was the first school in Albion Township. People known to have lived in New Albion in the 1850s and 1860s include Dr. Wright, Clifford Dawson, a Chesley and John Baker.

NEW JERUSALEM

The Village of New Jerusalem was founded on the West Fork of the Cedar River in Section 9 of Beaver Township. A dam was constructed across the West Fork just west of the town site, and a sawmill was built on the western bank. It made a very promising beginning and at one time contained a store and a number of residences. The name was later changed to Butler Rapids. The establishment of Willoughby, about a half mile west across the river, sapped the vitality of Butler Rapids and eventually brought about its extinction. The greater part of its population removed to Willoughby or elsewhere. Its houses were torn down, moved away or left to rot on their sites.

It is unclear where the name New Jerusalem came from. Some claim it was named after a traveling stage show, and others say it was named after the nationality of the man who built the mill on the West Fork.

NORTON'S CORNERS

Norton's Corners is the intersection of 270th Street and County Road T-55. From Shell Rock, take the Butler Center Road (T-45) west four miles to T-55 and go south two miles. This intersection was where the village of Norton's Corners was located as early as 1856. At one time, there was a school, a church (Bethel Chapel), Wait Creamery, a blacksmith and a store located on the banks of Dry Run Creek. There was no cemetery in this location; people used the Shell Rock Cemetery. There were not actually many houses built on the intersection; rather, the farmers from the area used the village to supply their needs. There are no known records of a post office ever being located here.

Mary Norton recalled that her husband's father and his father owned three corners of the intersection known as Norton's Corners. The general store and creamery were located on the fourth corner. The church was about a mile west of the intersection, according to *A Type of Foxfire History*.

As late as the 1970s, newspapers from both Shell Rock and Waverly printed a once-weekly column detailing the activities of Norton's Corners. There was a correspondent who collected the news from the other area farmers. Emma Dean collected the weekly news in the 1940s. People telephoned her to deliver their news for the column; they knew who to call to broadcast their news. Many weeks, the column detailed who visited whom, but other weeks there might be big news of a child graduating, military service, a new grandchild or even illnesses or death.

It is not known when the blacksmith, store and creamery ceased to exist, but the village remained bound by familiar ties. As late as the 1990s and into 2000, there were reunions held yearly for the children of the farmers from Norton's Corners.

Lyman Norton came to Iowa from Shabbona, Illinois, in the fall of 1854 by wagon train. On May 13, 1856, Lyman, his wife and their six children purchased land in Section 29 of Shell Rock Township, Butler County, Iowa, "with seventy dollars in hand," according to Butler County courthouse records. The first land Lyman and his son Edwin bought was east of Norton's Corners. Eventually, they owned about four hundred acres in the area of Norton's Corners. Edwin Norton was eighteen years old when they began purchasing land, and he lived his life working the land.

Lyman Norton enlisted in the Union army and served eleven months, going back to Shabbona, Illinois, in 1863. Two of his sons, Byron and William, enlisted and were killed in conflicts in Missouri in 1864. Edwin remained on the farm and married Mary Waters, whom he had met on the wagon train trip to Butler County in 1854. Their son, Byron Servetus Norton, lived on and farmed the land until his death in 1933 at the age of sixty-six.

In the 1930s, the Great Depression, poor weather and decreased farm yields claimed the land the Nortons' had lived on for seventy-seven years. Byron Servetus Norton had seven children, and all had left the farm except for twin sons Harry and Howard Norton. Following Byron's death, they sold the remaining land, livestock and machinery on December 12, 1933.

Edwin L. Norton, one of the first settlers in the area known as Norton's Corners. *Property of Byron James Norton, used with his permission.*

The following is from Hart's *History of Butler County, Iowa:*

> *For almost sixty years Edwin L.Norton has been a resident of Butler County and is one of its extensive landowners. His home place, known as the Oak Ridge Stock Farm, is located at Norton's Corners on Section 32, Shell Rock Township, and there he engages in raising high-grade stock, including horses, cattle and hogs. He has now traveled life's journey for seventy-five years and as one of the pioneer settlers of this locality, his memory forms a connecting link between the primitive past and the progressive present.*
>
> *A native of Ohio, he was born in Cuyahoga County, on the 15th of August, 1838, and is a son of Lyman and Hannah (Gates) Norton, who were also natives of the Buckeye State. In 1842, they removed to DeKalb County, Illinois, and in the fall of 1854 the father arrived in Butler County, Iowa, settling in the district which became known as Norton's Corners in Shell Rock Township. There he resided until 1862 when he went to Missouri, but after a short time returned to DeKalb County, Illinois, where*

his last days were spent, reaching the venerable age of eighty-four years. The mother also died in DeKalb County, but before the family removed to Iowa. The father afterward married again and his second wife died in DeKalb County. Lyman Norton was a farmer and also worked at the carpenter's trade to some extent. In antebellum days, he was a strong opponent of slavery and when the Republican Party was formed to prevent its further extension, he became one of its strong advocates.

In the family were three daughters and four sons born of the first marriage: Ann, who became the wife of Frank Stevens and is now a widow living in Shabbona, Illinois; Melissa, who became the wife of Alby (Mose) Robinson and died in the county; Edwin L, Byron and William, who enlisted in Missouri, for service in the Civil War, the former being killed in battle, while the latter was mortally wounded in a conflict and died a few days after reaching home; and LeRoy, who has been superintendent of schools during the greater part of his life and now makes his home in Michigan. There were also seven children born of the father's second marriage.

Edwin L. Norton was a youth of about fourteen years at the time of his mother's death, and in 1854, when sixteen years of age, he came with his father to Butler County, where he has since lived with the exception of a few months spent in Kansas. He has always followed farming and now owns about four hundred acres of rich and valuable land. His home is situated on Section 32, Shell Rock Township, and he has two hundred and forty acres on Sections 5 and 6, Beaver Township. The two farms are only about a half-mile apart. The purpose to which the home place is largely devoted has given to it the name of Oak Ridge Stock Farm, for here Mr. Norton raises high-grade stock, including cattle, horses and hogs. His political support is given to the Republican Party and he keeps well-informed on the questions and issues of the day but does not seek nor desire office, having always preferred to concentrate his energies upon his business affairs which, capably managed, have brought to him success.

In 1861, Edwin Norton was married to Miss Mary J. Waters, who was born in Cortland County, New York, in 1844, her parents being Servetus and Mercy (Helm) Waters, natives of Connecticut and New York respectively. They removed to DeKalb County, Illinois, when Mary J. Norton was ten years of age, and in 1858 came to this county, where both passed away when well advanced in years. The father died in 1892 in his ninetieth year and the mother when eighty-four years of age. They were the parents of seven children: Amos, who died in Oregon; Abner, who died in Denver, Colorado; Alzina, who became the wife of Olen Stevens and both died in Illinois; Joseph of Seattle, Washington; Julius, who was killed at the battle of Pleasant Hill while serving in the Civil War; and Mrs. Norton.

Four children were born unto Edwin and Mary J. Norton; Florence became the wife of M.G. Parks and died at the age of twenty-two years, leaving a daughter Blanche, who is now the wife of Milton Willey, of Shell Rock Township, by whom she has three children; Margaret and twins, born in December, 1913. Byron, the second member of the Norton family, resides upon and operates the home farm. He married Eva Church, who was born September 3, 1873, and died May 5, 1910. They became the parents of seven children: Earl, Madge, Lois, Ruth, Vera, and Harry and Howard, twins. Estella Norton, the third member of the family, became the wife of M.G. Parks of Albion Township (the same man her sister had married) and they have three children: Leland, Edith and Harland. Maude, the fourth member of the family, is the wife of Clyde Bolton, living on her father's farm in Beaver Township, and they have one son, Wayne.

No history of this county would be complete without mention of Edwin L. Norton, so long has he resided in this district. There were few white settlers living in Butler County at the time of his arrival and the Indians were still numerous in some sections. Land was largely unclaimed and uncultivated but the soil was naturally rich and productive and offered excellent opportunities to the farmer. Mr. Norton has lived to witness all the changes which have occurred—changes wrought by time and man, and he can relate many interesting incidents concerning the history of the county from pioneer times to the present.

Seth Dean owned the sawmill from about 1935 to 1950. The entire area of Norton's Corners was made up of black walnut, walnut, elm and burr oak trees. The sawmill was located in a thirty-acre stand of black walnut timber. Dean sold the wood from these trees, and the black walnut boards were highly prized.

Seth Dean also owned and operated a Case threshing machine for the Norton's Corners farmers. It was used for threshing oats. Threshing time was a big deal to everyone involved. Wherever the thresher went, the women followed. There were ten to twelve men to operate the threshing machine. This did not include the water boys (water was needed to cool the machine, the horses and the men) the local farmers and others who arrived to help or observe. The women planned and prepared huge meals. They had full

Happy Hour Club 1923

The Happy Hour Club, 1923. *Collection of Paul Franken, used with his permission.*

meals at lunch and suppertime, plus coffee in the morning and snacks in the afternoon. These midday breaks were full meals on their own. The women pitched in and assisted one another, just as the men did with threshing, according to Seth's daughter, Valena Dean.

Rosie Harms wrote about a club that began in the early part of the twentieth century and continues on into the twenty-first century. The Happy Hour Club is a Norton's Corners fixture. Two and three generations of women from the same family have belonged to it. This is mostly a social club, but members also assist when needed. The picture shown is from about 1923. Names written on the back are Mrs. Lynch, Elma Harms holding Wendell Harms, Mrs. Hanish, Mrs. Essex, Mrs. Green, Mrs. Lynch, Mrs. Nieman, Erma Dean, Addie Dean, Mrs. Bob Miller, Mrs. Jones and Elpha Waite. The children are Vernon Harms, Norma Harms, Sidney Dean, Jack Waite and Thelma Huntley.

Fannie Franken Albrecht recalls when electricity arrived in the Norton's Corners neighborhood. It was about 1943 or 1944, and this was an occasion for everyone.

There is a reference in a newspaper of a Norton's School as early as 1884. Norton's Corners School was built east of the intersection along Dry Run

Bethel Chapel Church, located a quarter mile west of Norton's Corners. It was used as a school when the schoolhouse burned down. *Collection of Paul Franken and Fannie Franken Albrecht.*

Creek. In 1923, classes were moved to Bethel Chapel, as the school building was in such poor condition from past flooding. In 1929, a fire started in the chapel from split shingles stacked next to the furnace. The shingles were used for kindling to start the fire. The fire started in the basement and spread quickly to the whole building, destroying it and the school records.

Following the fire, students were moved back to the old schoolhouse, which had been repaired. A short time later, in 1930, a new brick schoolhouse was built on the northeast corner of the intersection. It had a white tile roof and "fancy trim." This brick schoolhouse became the pride of Norton's Corners and was used for many neighborhood meetings and programs.

The Norton's Corners Schoolhouse was a large building as compared to other schools in the area. There was a full basement where the furnace and a portable stage were stored. It had red tile walls and a white slate roof. A pony shed was built in the northeast corner of the lot for the many ponies the students rode to school. There were separate outdoor toilets, one for boys and one for girls. A hedge surrounded the lot, which the students knew was their boundary when playing. There was a large swing set with many swings and a wooden teeter-totter. The Norton's Corners School had the largest enrollment of the schools in Shell Rock Township.

In 1946, Miss Rodman took the first- and second-grade classes on an exciting trip. The teacher's parents lived in Greene, in the northern part of Butler County. She made arrangements for them to travel by train to

Children from Norton's Corner School took a ride on a train in 1946. *Front row, left to right*: Howard White, Edwin Rodenbeck, Maryls Mixdorf and Donald Gersema, *Back row, left to right*: unknown, Ray Lindaman, unknown Sealman and Agnes Rindels. *Collection of Paul Franken and Fannie Franken Albrecht, used with their permission.*

Greene, have lunch with her parents and return to Shell Rock. This was the first train ride for the students. They left the Shell Rock depot, wild with anticipation. All brought up the subject of this train ride over sixty years after it occurred.

Maury Sutton attended the Norton's Corners School from 1949 to 1956. Maury writes,

> *My favorite story and memory involves our "hot lunch" during the winter months. On Monday, we had tomato soup in addition to whatever our mothers had packed us for lunch. I have no idea who provided the soup but the various families probably rotated. Then Friday it was mashed potatoes and butter day. We would all bring x number of peeled spuds. Mrs. Jackson would cook them on a hot plate and then use her mixer to make mashed potatoes. Since she was dealing with 30 to 60 potatoes, the mixer would always smell hot before she completed the task. We would all pass through the line with our bowls and Mrs. Jackson would ask us how many potatoes we had contributed. She would then spoon out the appropriate amount and*

Norton's Corners School. The brick building was the largest school in Butler County.
Collection of Paul Franken and Fannie Franken Albrecht, used with their permission.

I swear she would always finish with the right amount. We would then top this with butter brought from home, usually ¼ stick or more. Those were the pre-cholesterol days.

The school continued to function until 1962. At that time, Iowa State no longer issued High School Normal Training Certificates for teachers of rural schools. All rural schools in Iowa were closing. Thus, the Norton's Corners School closed, and the district paid tuition for the students to attend a town school. Norton's Corners' students were divided between Waverly–Shell Rock and New Hartford schools.

Mr. and Mrs. Walter Harms purchased the brick schoolhouse from Waverly–Shell Rock Schools in 1967. The building became home to the Assembly of God Chapel from the mid-1970s for several years.

The building was destroyed and the land is now a field owned by Richard Harms.

Teachers for Shell Rock Number 1—Norton's Corners School
1909–11—Mabel Dewey
1911–12—Jessie Wheat

1912–13—Mabel Dewey

1913–15—Nola Pierce

1915–16—Flora Fisk

1916–17—Helga Holm

1917–18—Mrs. Dora Tish

1918–19—Georgiana Eichhorn (thirty-two students enrolled, the second largest school in the county)

1919–20—no records

1920–21—Iola Watson

1921–22—Katharine Bolton

1922–23—Mildred Fleshner

1923–24—Katharine Bolton

1924–25—Frieda Spinner

1925–26—Nellie Jones

1927–28—Maud Williamson

1928–29—Lucille Clause

1929–30—Estella Van Dorn

1930–31—Genevieve Hunt

1931–33—Zoe Avery

1934–35—Sophia Garner

1935–36—Margaret Rosenwinkel

1936–37—Mildred Potter

1937–39—Ellen Mahoney

1939–43—Neva Miller (Mrs. Naube)

1943–47—Ethel Rodman
   assisted by Delors Hites

1947–56—Edna Jackson

PACKARD, PILOT ROCK, PROCTOR'S POND AND PROSPER

PACKARD

Packard is located on the corner of County Road T47 and Division Street, in Dayton Township, Section 22. This is another town that was founded because of the railroad passing through the area.

In 1883, Joseph purchased the land in Section 22. This town was known as Roots Siding in the beginning. In 1917, the population of the town was fifty-two. Packard's post office began in 1878 but was no longer in use in 2010.

A Methodist church was founded in 1914 and remains active. There is also a farmer's elevator in the town.

PILOT ROCK

Pilot Rock formed one of the most conspicuous landmarks upon the treeless, trackless prairie. This boulder, one of the largest in the state, measures thirty-eight feet in length, twenty-six feet in width and twelve feet in height above the ground. How much of it is buried beneath the surface is unknown. It is composed of a very hard gray granite similar in quality to many of the boulders of the surrounding territory and plainly coming originally from the same parent ledge in the faraway northland.

Pilot Rock, 2009. *Taken by Lester Homeister, used with his permission.*

In 1914, it stood on the farm of W.P. Miller in Section 22 of West Point Township. Miller's farm was named Pilot Rock Stock Farm. It is about three miles east of Bristow. Many early settlers used this rock to pilot themselves, as it was so large and could be seen easily, according to Hart's *History of Butler County, Iowa.* Jay and Sue Schrage now own and farm the land around Pilot Rock.

PROCTOR'S POND

Proctor's Pond is located in Albion Township, near New Hartford. In 1864, the area was split between Union loyalists and Rebel sympathizers. Many harsh words were thrown about, but nothing much happened until one day, the "brave boys in blue" were home on furlough from the Union army. The expressions of dislike for "Lincoln's hirelings" came to their notice. They traced the source of the animosity to Jonas Proctor and gathered at his farm. He was working in a wheat field, and they accosted him and demanded he "hurrah for Lincoln and the Union." Proctor refused, at which time the Union army soldiers grabbed a rail from a nearby fence and mounted Proctor upon it. They transported him to the nearby pond.

They came upon a man named Smith, who tried to defend Proctor, and Smith found himself upon the same rail. When they arrived at the pond, Smith shouted lustily for the Union and was allowed his freedom. Proctor continued to refuse and was ducked in the pond. Still refusing to comply, Proctor was ducked more times. Eventually, Proctor, sullen, silent and unable to express himself by only hand gestures, motioned that he would comply with the soldiers. This body of water has been called Proctor's Pond from that time, according to the *1883 Butler-Bremer County, Iowa History*.

PROSPER

Prosper was located in Fremont Township, Section 10. A post office was shown as being in this area from 1891 to 1900. Charles Skinner was the first postmaster. Others included William J. Simmens and Fergus D. Humbert. The Beaver Creek School was located in Section 4, just a half mile from the post office. The 1875 *Illustrated Historical Atlas of the State of Iowa* shows a store at Prosper.

OPLINGTON, ROOTS SIDING, SANDHILL AND SWANTON

OPLINGTON

Oplington was an early name of Eleanor. Aplington is also located close to where these towns were located.

ROOTS SIDING

Roots Siding was located in Dayton Township, Section 22. The present village of Packard is located about a half mile west of Roots Siding. A post office was in the area and was named Roots Siding from 1889 to 1903. The railroad ran near the area of Roots Siding.

The 1875 *Illustrated Historical Atlas of the State of Iowa* shows a blacksmith, general store, elevator and post office. The blacksmith shop opened in 1872. A C.W. Arkhill bought the general store, moved it next to the blacksmith and promoted a new town, named Arkhill. Supposedly, lots were selling, but no town was plotted and no houses were built. In 1889, a creamery was at Roots Siding, and a cheese factory was built in 1901. It became known for its Swiss, American and brick cheeses, according to the *Butler County Cemetery Records*. The 1917 population of Packard was twenty-six.

SANDHILL

Sandhill was located along the railroad line between Greene and Packard, in Section 18 in Fremont Township. No mention of a post office has been found. It was probably a town that came to being because of the railroad.

SWANTON

The village of Swanton was located in the northwest quarter of Section 11 of Albion Township. The village began in 1856 when the Swanton Post Office was moved to this location. The post office had previously operated out of various homes in the area. The post office was discontinued on October 15, 1902, and the town ceased to exist soon after.

The village was platted with twenty-four blocks, with the northern tier passing into Jefferson Township. The township line later became Main Street. Other east–west streets were Kossuth and Buchanan. The north–south streets were Lemont, Broadway, Senecca, Washington and East. The village had a store, a creamery, a blacksmith shop, an icehouse, a sawmill, a post office and an interdenominational church. The Swanton School was just north of the town. All the businesses were located around a public square, as described in the *Parkersburg Eclipse* by Vopal Youngburg.

The *1883 Butler-Bremer County, Iowa History* relates how the post office came to Swanton. Mrs. Lorenzo Perry, who lived a mile east of New Albion, walked to Cedar Falls for her mail. On her return, she brought the official documents establishing a post office under the name of Swanton, named for Mrs. Perry's hometown of Swanton, Vermont. Jacob Brown was commissioned the first postmaster, the office being kept in his home.

Postmasters included Jacob Brown, who began his duties on April 22, 1859, with Isaac K. Carpenter taking over the responsibilities in 1861. Flekker C. Putman became postmaster on November 18, 1862; George Murphy took over on December 12, 1864; and James W. Heoard assumed the position on April 2, 1868. Henry Brown became postmaster on October 9, 1868; Hiram W. Churchille took over on January 7, 1859; and Lewis Hovey assumed the duties on May 9, 1871. Marcina S. Hovey became postmistress on April 30, 1877; Elias Hovey was installed in the job on June 18, 1879; Haiter D. Hambert took over the position on February 5, 1896; and May Caywood, the last postmistress, was installed on April 27, 1898.

Vanished Towns of the Cedar Valley

Swanton School with students in front of it. *Collection of Vopal Youngberg, used with her permission.*

The post office was moved to the general store sometime in the mid-1860s. This was located on the south line of Section 11, a half mile south of the Swanton School. Mrs. Olive Johnson brought mail to this new office twice a week until a rural route was established out of New Hartford. Rural Free Delivery began about 1896.

About 1901, the Swanton School (or Albion Number 7) was built on the corner of George Schreurs's farm. This school operated until 1955. Some of the teachers were Elizabeth Schreurs Perrin, Rose Schreurs Jennings, Helen Lashbrook Becker, Dorothy Perrin Mason, Esther Perrin Becker, Agnes Essex Wessel, Donna Bullis and Viola Jarstad. Winnie Cain taught in Swanton from 1951 through 1955. The schoolhouse was moved to Henry Capper's farm when the school closed.

Across the road from the Swanton School was the meetinghouse of the Mystic Toilers. Very little is known about this fraternal society other than that at one time it did business in cemetery monuments. The monuments have the inscription "erected by the Mystic Toilers." Obituaries of some Swanton citizens mention that they were members of the Mystic Toilers Society.

In the early 1900s, the Mystic Toilers abandoned their building, and it was moved to the southeast corner of Section 11, east of the store and creamery, where it became the Community Sunday School Building. Ministers from nearby towns held services there for many years.

The grocery store was owned and operated by several different men over the years. Among them were Albert Eliason, Fred Sherman, Will Chapman, Gus Hendricks and Okke Schneiderman. The store closed in 1930.

A blacksmith shop was important to each village. Some of the smithies who worked in the Swanton blacksmith shop were Fred Johnson, Tony Sorenson, George Hansen and Carl Juel.

The creamery operated for many years, closing in the late 1920s. Among the known butter makers were Otis Courbat, Will Graham and Harry Chapman.

An icehouse was significant in each community prior to the installation of electricity, which occurred in Iowa by about 1920. In Swanton, the icehouse

Swanton, 2008. *Taken by Diane Van Mill, used with her permission.*

was located next to the creamery. Esther Becker recalled what a gala day it was when the farmers "paraded" by on their way to the West Fork to cut ice to fill the icehouse. The West Fork was about three miles north of Swanton. Ice harvest began when the ice was twelve inches thick. The snow was cleared off the ice, and the ice was marked in blocks. An ice saw was used to cut through the ice and turn it into blocks. Horses were brought onto the ice to haul the blocks back to Swanton. The blocks were stacked with sawdust between them to keep the chunks from freezing together. Sawdust covered the entire stack to insulate it until it was used during the summer.

The populace bought the blocks of ice to make ice cream during the summer. Those with means used an icebox for food storage. With the installation of rural electricity, there was another business with no use, and the icehouse fell into disuse.

People known to have lived in or around Swanton include F.L. Brown (1895), Fred Sherman, the Jaquis family, Will Chapman, Tony Sorenson and Harry Chapman.

There was nothing left to see of Swanton as of 2008. Houses had been moved or destroyed, and the town was returning to farm fields.

TAYLOR'S RIDGE, UNION RIDGE AND VILMAR

TAYLOR'S RIDGE

Taylor's Ridge was located in Beaver Township, near to both Beaver Grove and Bear Grove. The post office existed only a short time before moving to New Hartford, as told in the *Butler County Cemetery Records.*

UNION RIDGE

Union Ridge had a post office in Pittsford Township, Section 20. Isaac Stover, a resident of the eastern edge of Franklin County, wrote to the post office department and succeeded in securing the establishment of a post office at a town named Union Ridge in 1856. It was located about four miles northwest of Dumont. The Union Ridge Post Office was not located on any mail route, so the postmaster was obliged to carry the mail himself, sometimes on foot, and other times the patrons of the office would hire someone to carry the mail once a week. The Union Ridge office was supplied from the village of Geneva, in Franklin County.

James Harlan was appointed in 1862 postmaster and held the office until 1868. By that time, a regular mail route had been established, and mail was delivered at Union Ridge twice each week. The Union Ridge Post Office lasted twenty-one years, until 1877, making it one of the longest-serving of Butler County's early post offices, according to *the Butler County Cemetery Records.*

VILMAR

Vilmar is located in Coldwater Township, Section 35. St. John's Lutheran Church in Vilmar was established in November 1879. Prior to the church being built, services were held in the Prange Schoolhouse, which was two miles southeast of the church's current location. The church was built in 1883 and enlarged in 1902. During World War I and into the 1920s, there was much discussion about changing the language of the church from German to English. During World War I, everything German speaking was suspect. Many services were held in "high" German into the 1950s.

The year 1937 was the first time there was no resident pastor. A parsonage was built in 1938 at a cost of $5,200, and a minister was recruited. In 1881, a spot on the Fred Steere farm, about one and a half miles from the church, was chosen as the Vilmar Cemetery. The church continues to flourish, as discussed in the *Centennial of St. John's Evangelical Lutheran Church*.

The name of Vilmar was chosen by the Reverend Conrad Weltner after his Professor Vilmar in Germany.

In 1880, a house was built near the Stolte store. About 1900, a creamery was built in the area, and this flourished until after World War I. The store remained active until about this same time. In 1917, there were twenty-one people living in Vilmar. In the 1950s, a merchandise store and creamery were located just east of the church. The store was run by a Mr. and Mrs. Meyer. Today, the church is the only building remaining in Vilmar.

Vilmar grocery store, 1913. Butler County Centennial Fair Book.

Vilmar Church. Centennial of St. John's Lutheran Church, Vilmar, *1979*.

WAVERLY JUNCTION, WEST POINT, WILLOUGHBY AND WILSON'S GROVE

WAVERLY JUNCTION

Although this village was located in Bremer County, it is included because it was so close to Shell Rock and many people from this area traveled to Shell Rock for their business. It was located about five miles east and south of Shell Rock. Follow East Washington Street out of Shell Rock, which becomes a gravel road called Woods Avenue. Go south about one mile and at the next intersection turn east on 250th Street. Drive another two miles, and the road will curve south and become Badger Avenue. Go one and a quarter miles to a T intersection with 265th Street. West Point Cemetery is on a hill on the west side of the road. Turn to the left, or east, on 265th Street, and at the railroad crossing vicinity is where Waverly Junction was located, according to the *Bremer County 150th Anniversary Celebration Book*.

Waverly Junction was located in Section 29 of Jackson Township in Bremer County. The village was named this because the railroad spur ran from the main line of the Rock Island Railroad to Waverly. From 1910 to 1920, five round trips ran daily between the Junction (as it was known) and Waverly. Freight cars were the only rail transport until the 1940s.

Stockyards, a store and a post office were also located here. The post office was established on April 21, 1902, with William H. Veza as postmaster.

Farmers in the area found it convenient to use the train to ship cattle and hogs to Chicago. They used Howard McCaffree's platform scale to weigh their cattle.

An important event in Waverly Junction and Iowa history occurred when President Howard Taft visited Waverly Junction during the presidential

A gathering of men to hear President Howard Taft speak in Waverly Junction. *Bremer County genweb.*

campaign of 1910. The president's train made a thirty-minute stop at the junction, where a large group of people greeted him.

As automobiles became more common and farmers could transport their cattle to market themselves, the use of the junction died out in the 1940s. The cemetery is located on a hill overlooking the town.

WEST POINT

West Point is located in West Point Township, Section 19. George Lash and Henry Early first platted the town, consisting of ten acres on Section 18 and ten acres on Section 19.

Julius Huffman erected a frame log house and used it to sell goods for about two years, beginning in 1860. Over the years, the town has housed several general stores, a drugstore, several blacksmith shops, a hotel, churches and schools.

The first school in West Point Township was taught during the winter of 1859–60 at the home of Thomas Hewitt by Miss Mary Rich, with fifteen students in attendance. The schoolhouse was located one mile east of the town.

In 1876, the name of West Point was changed to Bristow because there was already another West Point in the state of Iowa. In 1881, the town was incorporated, and elections were held to fill offices. Bristow is an unincorporated collection of homes at the time of this writing. The school has consolidated with Allison to become the Allison-Bristow School District. There continues to be a post office in Bristow as of 2010.

WILLOUGHBY

Willoughby, platted in the southwest quarter of Section 9 of Beaver Township, was laid out in 1855. The proprietors were men by the name of Cameron and McClure, according to minutes at the Butler County Courthouse. This plat was recorded in the minute book of the county court, September 9, 1856. These men built the first house in 1855, and G.W. Daniels occupied it.

In the fall of 1855, the Cornwell brothers opened a store and stocked general merchandise. They operated the store until 1864, when they sold the contents to a man from Clear Lake. The building was divided and part sold to O.W. McIntosh, who operated a hotel, with the remainder of the building being sold to B. Haskins, who lived in the building.

The Cornwell brothers opened a blacksmith shop in 1856. They also built and operated a hotel from that same year until 1860, when they sold it to J.B. Gordon. The hotel was a regular stopping place on the route from Cedar Falls to Algona and enjoyed many visitors during the years before a railroad

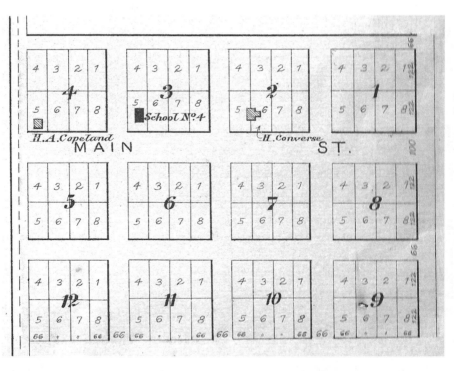

Willoughby village layout. *1906 plat book, printed by the* Times-Republican, *Marshalltown, Iowa.*

penetrated the county. Following Gordon, Robert Olmstead, O.W. McIntosh and H.D. Burnett owned the hotel. The hotel functioned until 1879.

The post office opened in 1855 with G.W. Daniels as the first postmaster. Other postmasters were David Diltz, Samuel Fetters, B. Haskins, O.D. Olmstead, R. Stanley, George Burnett and H.D. Burnett. The post office was discontinued prior to rural delivery reaching this area. Mail arrived twice weekly until 1883.

The first Butler County Fair was held in Willoughby in 1856. The only mention of it was found in the *1883 Butler-Bremer County, Iowa History*. It is believed the fair was held in Willoughby for two years and then moved to other towns, with no town holding the fair for more than two years in a row. Due to the temporary nature of the fairgrounds and lack of permanent buildings, the success of the fair was limited, according to the *Butler County Centennial Fair Book*.

Miss Hannah Ensign taught at the first school during the winter of 1857–58 at the home of Mr. King. The first schoolhouse was erected in 1861. The Protestant Methodist Church was organized in 1870 but only lasted about two years.

The population of Willoughby was shown as fifty-eight settlers in 1855.

By 1883, only two houses remained standing apart from the schoolhouse, and Willoughby had ceased to exist, according to the *1883 Butler-Bremer County, Iowa History*.

WILSON'S GROVE

Wilson's Grove was located in Bennezette Township, Section 15. It was named after Milton Wilson, a pioneer of 1857. He was one of the first county supervisors elected in 1859, serving a term of one year, and was reelected in 1860.

Wilson's Grove was a post office established in April 1878. Milton Wilson was postmaster, with the office at his house on Section 15. Mail arrived once a week from Greene during the first year and, after that, twice a week from Sheffield. The office was discontinued in the fall of 1880, according to the *Bennezette Township History*.

Closing

What caused the "death" of these towns? The simplest explanation is the development of the railroads. If the rail line did not go near one of these towns, the village began to die as people moved to a community where there was a railroad. The railroad allowed easy communication with the outside world, an affordable and close vehicle to market the products the farms produced and brought more people to the neighborhood. Rail service ensured the growth and permanence of the town.

In 1854, the first train reached the Mississippi River at Rock Island, Illinois, coming from the East Coast. Ferryboats carried the freight and passengers across the river to the cities in Iowa. In 1855, the first engine was ferried across the Mississippi from Illinois. Just one year later, a wooden bridge spanned the wide river so that freight and passenger rail cars could travel across.

Building railroads cost a lot of money. The railroad from Davenport to Iowa City cost $15,000 per mile in the 1850s. (This figure translates to $340,000 in 2003 dollars.) To encourage railroad companies to build, Congress passed laws that gave land to companies that promised to build railroads. The four railroad companies had just begun to build across the state when the Civil War interrupted progress.

After the Civil War, railroad companies began selling their land grants to get the money needed for rail construction. In 1867, the first railroad to cross the Missouri River to Iowa was completed. Smaller railroad companies soon linked the towns and cities of Iowa with the mainline railroads all across the state.

There were three rail lines traversing Butler County. The following is the course and location of the various railroads:

- The Burlington, Cedar Rapids and Northern Railway, built in 1871, entered Butler County from the southeast and followed the Shell Rock Valley across the northeastern part of the county.
- The Iowa Division of the Illinois Central Railroad, constructed in 1865, crossed the county from east to west through the southern tier of townships.
- The Dubuque and Dakota Railroad, graded through in 1875 by the Iowa and Pacific Railroad Company, crossed the county in the same direction, entering with the Shell Rock River. It followed the valley northward to Clarksville, where it made an abrupt curve and crossed the county in the second tier of townships from the north. This company failed, and the road came into the possession of the Dubuque and Dakota Railroad Company. The track was laid and trains were running through Butler County in 1879.

The railroads provided a huge opportunity for producers in Iowa to reach distant markets, helping to spur the economy. Unlike the steamboats and overland trails, the railroads functioned year-round, allowing for travel of goods and passengers to and from the state. Iowa's agricultural economy was greatly influenced by the growth of the railroads.

Railroads greatly impacted the lives of Iowans. Life would never be the same for most people after the railroads came to town. Railroads brought new products to people living on isolated farms and in small towns. The parts of Iowa where only a few settlers had been living began to fill with people. Railroads became the key to the growth and success of towns and cities. The places the railroads bypassed remained small or sometimes faded away.

So what happened to the towns? Aside from the location of the railroads, the most common reasons that villages ceased to exist were that their sources of income or water were exhausted, disasters occurred, their post offices closed or they were not given county seat status.

Many of the sites were only towns as far as the post office was concerned. They had no businesses or other commerce. Sometimes there was not even a collection of houses to signify the "town." The house that served as the post office was on a route from one larger town to another; thus, the neighbors petitioned to become a post office so their mail could be dropped closer to their homes. Once the mail service no longer stopped at their location, the town name was no longer used, and there is nothing remaining to show that a town might have once stood there.

Yet the town sites or other geographic landmarks are still referred to by longtime citizens of the area. Directions are given listing a large rock or lake. A church that is all that remains from a town is still referred to by the town's name. This book has been researched to preserve the memory of these lost towns. Iowa has more towns than most other states and is proud that their stories are kept alive.

All the towns were founded with dreams of greatness. No one can imagine the difficulties the settlers undertook to live on the frontier. Every village was important to the surrounding area. The stories of these towns are part of Iowa's history.

CEMETERY RECORDS

ANTIOCH CEMETERY

The Antioch Church, three miles east of Clarksville, was demolished by a windstorm on a Saturday afternoon, March 24, 1915. It was first dedicated in February 1873. The congregation, then known as the Christian Church, was once among the strongest churches in the county, having over five hundred members living in northeastern townships. The Reverend T.R. Hansberry was the pastor who assisted in the organization of the church. On November 6, 1858, records show it is stated, "The members of the Antioch congregation met for the purpose of setting apart their respective officers." They proceeded to elect to the eldership Wm. McBarnard and Charles S. Martin; to the deaconship James Hodgson and James R. Taylor; and to the clerkship John T. Davis.

At its organization, the church had no building in which to hold its services and met in the old schoolhouse known as Number 5 about forty rods south of the Antioch Cemetery.

On June 29, 1872, John Saddler and his wife, Elizabeth, conveyed to the trustees of the Christian Church a half acre of ground about thirty rods east of the cemetery, and upon that land the church was erected. This was the building in which the congregation held its services until 1891. The building was built at the cost of $1,200. On April 18, 1891, the trustees of the church sold it to the Antioch Union Church Association for $250. The Antioch

Union Church Association held meetings in the building for many years, but with the coming of the automobile and the removal of most of the original families of the community, church services were discontinued. Christmas programs and Memorial Day services were held in the building for many years. These served as old settlers' reunions and were well attended.

The cemetery is still being used and holds the graves of many of those old settlers who were active in the Antioch Church so many years ago. It is divided in two sections, the westernmost part being the old addition and the eastern side, the new addition. Kenny Forry or Karen Kuker is thought to be in charge.

ANGELL, Herald S. Aug. 24, 1910 to Sept 10, 1910 E-18
Angell family stone E-16
Ella M. 1892–1959 E-16
Elmer E. CO D 129th Infantry 33 Div E-16
Nancy E. 1890–1918 E-16
Mother 1856–1943 E-16
Lee N. Father 1852–1933 E-16
Angell family stone W-3
John W. Jan 2, 1856 Dec 14, 1922 W-3
Charles H. 1825–1909 W-3
Ellanor R. 1828–1898 W-3

BARKELEW, Erskine 1864–1949 E-30
Charles L. 1861–1950 E-30
Frank W. 1876–1951 E-30
William S. 1871–1952 E-30

BECKER, Louise Anna Nov 19, 1867 to Mar 15, 1868 W-8

BILHIMER, Infant son of H. & C. no dates W-26
Malinda H. wife of C. Bilhimer Dec 6, 1863 20y 8m 12d W-26
Christopher July 4, 1835 to July 1, 1903 Civil War Veteran W-26

BOECKMAN, Ann 1914–1974 E-45

BOLIN, Ida B.A. daug of W. & M.A. Bolin Mar 6, 1896 to Nov 5, 1901 E-7
Baby Ruth daug of G.W. & M.A. Bolin Jan 29, 1895 E-7
George W. 1854–1931 E-7
Margaret A. 1858–1948 E-7
Cora daug 1899–   E-7
Blanche daug 1890–1964 E-7
John C. 1865–1947 E-8
Mollie Jan 6, 1866 Jan 1903 E-8

CALVERT, Mamie no dates W-11
Adam no dates W-11

CARPENTER, Myrna A. Mar 26, 1885 to Oct 6, 1885 W-21

CASS, F.D. 1843–1923 E-14

CLOUKEY, Archie M. Feb 2, 1883 ly 7m 18d
(child of J. & M. Cloukey) W-35
Ira C. Mar 10, 1887 2y 5m 20d W-35
Ira (separate stone) W-35
Lorin A. Apr 18, 1874 ly 7m ld W-35
Lorin (separate stone) W-35

CRIPPEN, Clarissa 1834–1904 Mother W-29
Alonzo B. Jan 19, 1878 60y 6m 2d W-29
Father (separate stone) W-29

CROSS, Wilber J. son of S.C. & P.A. Cross
Sept 13, 1880 13Y 9m 24d W-43
"O Brother First to leave our bond, Lifes song as yet unsung. While gray hairs gather
    on our brow
Thou art forever young."
Infant son July 14, 1879 W-34

DEPUEW, Ila M. Mother 1897–   E-31
Earl Father 1887–1984 Veteran E-31

ENGEL, Dorothy 1914–   E-35
Walter G. 1915–   E-35
Franziska 1877–1957 W-36
August 1861–1947 W-36
Engle, Theodore 1905–1929 W-9

EPHRAIN, Gust no dates E-17

EPLEY, Floyd owner of E-46 no stones

FASSETT, Rueben Nov. 19, 1835 to Mar 7, 1916 W-46
Polly Philinda Taylor Apr 16, 1843 to Dec 29, 1883 W-46
Mother W-46
Father W-46

FISHER, Betty JoAnn 1937–1984 Funeral Home Marker E-37
Mitzie Larae 1959–1959 Funeral Home Marker E-37
Dorotha L. 1912–   E-37
Arthur, W. 1906–1969 E-36
Marcy A. 1974–1974 Funeral Home Marker E-36
Evelyn M. 1919–1968 E-33
Mildred E. 1929–1952 E-25
Clara 1911–   E-25
Louise M. 1908–   E-25
Clara E. Mother 1885–1971 E-25
Henry J. Father 1880–1957 E-25
Alfred O. In Memory of Captain Alfred Fisher 1903–1942 E-24
Royal H. 1924–1937 Boy Scout E-24

FLESHNER, Jennie L. 1882–1967 E-22

FOLSOM, Dave Mack 1904–1967 E-24

FORD Emma Oct 25, 1852 Aug 15, 1901 W-12

FRANKLIN, Irwin J. 1876–1947 E-13
Ida C. 1889–1939 E-13

FULLER, Edwin A. Mar 4, 1868 Nov 5 1902 E-14
Harriet J. Nov 18, 1833 Sept 10, 1908 E-14
Edwin (separate stone) E-14

GARNER, Kenneth 1916-1975 Funeral Home Marker

GIBSON, Harold son of G.A. & A. Gibson Mar. 18, 1895 1Y 7m W-55

GILLES, Lawrence son of E.W. & Sarah Gilles Sept 6, 1894 5y 2m W-21

GOUGHENOUR, owner of W-5 on which the following can be found: Wooden cross
    no writing W-5
Cement Marker no writing W-5
Two wooden crosses no writing W-5

GRAPP, Augusta Sieling 1869–1944 E-10

GRIGG, Mittie Hall Apr 14, 1870 to June 11, 1917 W-30

GRAY, James F. son of R. & M. Gray Jan 11, 1821 ly 1 or 11m 15d W-32

Guy, Infant son of W.O. & R.J. Aug 22, 1873 W-32
Olive May daug of W.O. & R.J. Feb 20, 1870 W-32

Habermann, Bernice 1889–1974 W-1
Carl F. 1880–1951 W-1
Erma 1927 W-1
Karl F. Iowa First Lieutenant Infantry Korea
May 19, 1929 to Sept 15, 1971 W-1
Augusta 1840–1918 W-1
Carl 1845–1887 W-1
Lillian B. Mother 1874–1956 W-56
Rogar 1911–1922 W-56
A.H. Father 1874–1934 W-56

Hall family stone W-30
John R. Feb 6, 1855 Mar 30, 1921 W-30
Mary J. Aug 29, 1841 Dec 7, 1884 W-30
Ada Ellen daug of J.R. & M.J. Hall Mar. 4, 1869 2y 6m 29d W-30

Hanner, Emma 1844–1912 W-48
Fred CO B 24th NY Cavalry W-48
Wooden cross no information W-48

Harris, Burt 1886–1933 Funeral Home Marker E-33
Clarence 1912–1933 Funeral Home Marker E-33
Claud 1919–1933 Funeral Home Marker E-33
Mary A. 1863–1936 Funeral Home Marker E-33
George I. 1875–1938 Funeral Home Marker E-33

Hickman, Mathew Apr 18, 1886 76y 8m 22d W-40

Hodgson, Briget Mother Nov 15, 1915 E-12
Asa July 19, 1850 to Oct 30, 1901 E-1
Ruvira Walter 1856–1940 (second stone with same inscriptions) E-1
Fannie Nov 7, 1864 W-12
John June 12, 1858 W-12
John son of James and Elizabeth Sept. 1, 1863 4y 8m 23d W-27
Infant son of James and Elizabeth Dec. 8, 1859 W-27
James Mar 18, 1868 46y 8m W-27
John no dates W-29
Martha 1867–1920 W-29
Clarissa 1834–1904 W-29

Holzschul, Otto May 14, 1873 Sept 17, 1903 W-37
Hattie July 5, 1882 Nov 5, 1904 child of A. & T. W-37

Otto separate stone W-37
Hattie separate stone W-37
Alvin 1878–1952 W-37
Mother 1850–1927 W-37
Father 1842–1932 Civil War Veteran W-37

HOPKINS, Calista D. wife of H.W. Hopkins Oct 10, 1868?? Stone broken at the age
 line W-25

HUISMEN, Dick W. 1913–1975 E-47
Ruby L. 1916–   parents of William, Donald, Gary and Linda E-47
Tillie 1906–1983 E-44
Edward 1904–   parents of Eddina E-44

HULBERT, Father Pearl L. 1897–1962 E-34
Mother Vesta M. 1898–1971 E-34

HUNT, Minnie L. daug of I. & A. Mar 5, 1870 W-10

INGERSOLL, Stanley E. 1899–1975 E-38
Alma L. 1903–1977 parents of Dorothy, Geneva and Judith E-38

JOHNSON, Alonzo Jan 21, 1881 69y 6m 22d W-4

KIMMINS, Cynthia A. wife of John Feb 24, 1891
60y 3m 20d W-28
Cynthia separate stone W-28
John Feb 28, 1819 Mar 17, 1894 85y W-28
John separate stone W-28

KRATCHMER Helen I. 1907–   E-41
John W. 1898–1979 E-41

KRUCKERBERG, William 1893–1949 WWI W-49
Maria 1901–1931 W-49

LUMM, Ina V. Mother 1876–1952 E-31
Jesse E. Father 1855–1947 E-31
Minnie 1897–1954 E-26
Roland 1895–1970 E-26
Robert Lee 11-30-1937 to 2-21-1938 E-26

LYLE, Olive wife of J.M. Feb 17, 1873 44y 1m 15d W-33

MAJOR, William 1842–1928 W-27
Elizabeth 1823–1927 W-27

MARKLER, Markle Sarah M. wife of Geo. S. Oct 5, 1827–Dec 4, 1904 E-21

MARQUAND, Verto L. 1906–   E-28
Ruth E. 1908–   parents of Mary Ellen E-28

MARTIN, Rebecca wife of W.C. Aug 9, 1846 Oct 13, 1904 E-10
W.C. 1842–1941 E-10
John Henry 1873–1937 E-10

MEHMEN, Ella 1891–1928 E-17
William I. 1881–1964 E-17

MOON, Mary M. wife of Elijah Moon 1847–1874 W-28

MOORE, R.G. Mar 19, 1835 no date of death W-2
Mary April 15, 1832 Apr 20, 1900 W-2
Footstone no inscription W-2
Allen Jan 1, 1883 23Y 3m 14d W-2

MORROW, ?? daug of T. & M.E. Mar 24, 1878 5y 3m 13d "Budded on Earth, to
   bloom in heaven." W-15

NELSON, Mary R.N. wife of C.R. Nelson Dec 1869 W-10
Amanda daug of W. & L. Searles Sept 6, 1838 to Sept 8, 1891 52y 11m 23d W-31
S.M. 1861–1937 W-40

NORDMAN, Lewis F. 1889–1970 Father W-37
Lulu L. 1892–1968 Mother W-37

NUSZ, Nellie A. 1858–1944 W-40
Lewis Jan 13, 1856 June 7, 1900 44y 4m 24d W-40

PAUL, Henry 1904–1980 E-40
Vada 1908–   E-40
Wooden cross no name or dates E-40

PERKINS, Josie 1880–1960 E-6
Mable lm E-6

READ, John E. Oct 22, 1877 40y 2m 16d Civil War Veteran W-14
John W. 1852–1866 W-28

SADLER, T.E. 1858–1935 W-33
Martha 1861–1929 W-33
John E. 1881–1938 W-33

Elizabeth wife of John 1817–1874 W-33
Martha wife 1861–1929 (second stone) W-33
T.E. 1858–1935 (second stone) W-33

SCOTT, Eugene Iowa Private Sup Co 101 Infantry WWI Apr 8, 1893 May 20, 1971
    E-15
Frances D. Feb 13, 1899 Nov 22, 1983 E-15
Darlys N. 1928 E-15

SEARLES, Mrs. Lorenzo Ross wife of Wm. Searles Apr 2, 1808 Mar 28, 1885 77y
    11m 6d W-31

SHAW, Sarah J. 1854–1938 W-17
Zachariah T. 1851–1929 W-17
Lela M. daug of Z.T. & S.J. Jan 2, 1878 2y 10m 15d W-17

SIELING, Karolina July 2, 1844 May 17, 1910 E-11
Carl Oct 25, 1839 Apr 28, 1933 E-11
Carl Jr. 1872–1951 E-11
Father separate stone E-11
Mother separate stone E-11

SINRAM, Fred 1883–1872 E-32
May 1887–1956 E-32

SKINNER, W.M. 1859–1904 E-20
Robert N. Mar 15, 1829 Feb 14, 1902 W-6
Father separate stone W-6
Mary H. Oct 13, 1834 Feb 10, 1911 W-6
Mother separate stone W-6
Wooden cross on W-6 no name or dates
John Mar 24, 1821 at Cornwall, England Mar 15, 1901 W-6

SPAFFORD, Alice wife of H.G. Feb 19, 1889 28y 11m 7d W-13

SWAN, Clara Belle Mar 4, 1865 to Apr 24, 1938 W-13
Elizabeth wife of M.M. Swan Jan 11, 1892 63y 6m W-19
H.M. Jan 12, 1884 63y 7m 5d W-19

THOMPSON family stone W-38
Eldon Earl 1905–1929 W-38
Grace E. 1885–1978 W-38
Ray B. 1883–1948 W-38
Kenneth O. 1909–   W-38
Luella A. 1915–   W-38

VAN SLYKE, Infant son Feb 23, 1901 E-2
B.R. small stone no dates E-2
L.P. small stone no dates E-2
Elizabeth daug of P. Apr 27, 1888 12y 11m 12d W-13
Three upright cement spears no names or dates, on lot owned by P. Van Slyke W-13
Wooden cross on W-13 no name or dates
James G. born in Little Falls, N.Y. Mar 2, 1802 died at Clarksville, Iowa May 8, 1885 W-54

WALRATH, George F. son of Franklin and Louisa Oct 8, 1880 25y 2m 8d W-12
George separate stone W-12
Wooden cross on W-12 no name or dates
Mary Sept 12, 1856 to Feb 21, 1911 W-12
Louisa Mother Sept 17, 1837 to Mar 23, 1923 W-12
Vernon son of F.W. & E. 1883 1883 W-18
Walrath family stone W-34

WALSH, Letitia Krapp Dec 31, 1815 to Jan 30, 1899 W-53
Thomas Jan 1, 1808 to Feb 11, 1884 W-53

WALTER, H.E. Jan 11, 1860 Nov 26, 1935 E-1
Charlie Jan 15, 1867 to Sept 10, 1952 E-1
Phelenia E. Nov 30, 1870 to July 12, 1920 E-1

WEILAND, Harold E. Sp 3 US Army Korea Oct 15, 1933–May 30, 1983 E-39
Leslie J. God Bless our Daug Mar 25, 1960 to Jan 7, 1962 E-39
Robert 1944–1958 E-38
Walter 1890–1968 E-38

WHEATON, John A. son of W.J. & E. June 2, 1873 18y 2m 20d W-31

WILDEBOER, Francis MSG US Army Korea Jan 9, 1917 Feb 25, 1981 E-27
David 1884–1953 E-27
Jennie 1896–1979 E-27

WILLIAMS, Will Oct 31, 1838 Aug 30, 1951 W-20
Leah wife of H. Oct 8, 1826 Jan 18, 1905 W-20
Mother separate stone W-20
Williams, Henry Apr 1903 78y 11m 15d W-20
Father separate stone W-20
Eldora July 27, 1877 Feb 21, 1939 W-20

WRIGHT family stone E-9
Florence, 1891–1904 E-9
May E. Mother 1869–1929 E-9
Dodo J. Father 1863–1944 E-9

YOST, Ivan G. Private. US Army WWI Aug 15, 1901 Mar 10, 1977 E-29
Edwin William Iowa TE2 US Navy Nov 2, 1929 Dec 16, 1967 E-29

Records from this cemetery were kept but are not complete. The following is a list
of lot numbers and owners on which wooden or cement markers without names
can be found.

E-40 Henry Paul: 1 wooden cross
E-3 Geo. Harris: 4 wooden crosses and 1 wooden cross, with names
W-5 Goughenour: 3 wooden crosses and 1 cement marker
W-6 R. Skinner 1 wooden cross
W-13 P. Van Slyke: 4 wooden crosses
W-12 Walrath: 1 wooden cross
W-43 S.G. Cross: 1 wooden cross
W-52 S.M. Knapp: 1 wooden cross
W-51 J. Perkins: 5 wooden crosses
W-52 A. Engle: 5 wooden crosses

BUTLER CENTER CEMETERY

The Butler Center Cemetery is located in the northeast quarter of Section
18 of Jefferson Township, three miles south of Allison and one mile east of
Highway 14 on County Road C45. This cemetery was a town cemetery for
Butler Center. Its first burial was in 1865. In 1870, it was under the jurisdiction
of the Jefferson Township Trustees. Later, the cemetery was transferred to
the Butler Center Cemetery Association, which was incorporated in 1917.

In 1950, the Butler County auditor was assigned as trustee for the small
cemetery. In 1962, the unused eastern half of the property owned by the
association was sold to the State College of Iowa (now the University of
Northern Iowa) for use as a natural prairie reserve.

In 2008, Robert Jannsen was sexton, and Donald Henrichs dug the graves.
Burials are current only through 1998.

BACKER, Gretja J. Enninga (Lot 134), wife of Heere, b. July 27, 1857; d. Mar. 8, 1903
Heere F. (Lot 134), 1855–1929
Heere F. (Lot 134), 1895–1923
Siefke J.H. (Lot 134), 1881–1913

Butler Center Cemetery. *Taken by Linda Betsinger McCann, 2010.*

BAILEY, Martin (Lot 21) C.W.; father, b. Nov. 7, 1819; d. Sept. 27, 1885; "They are at rest."
Mary A. Clark (Lot 21), mother, wife of Martin, b. Oct. 26, 1828; d. July 28, 1885; "They are at rest."

BALDWIN, Almy (Lot 141), daug. of S.M. & C., d. Apr. 4, 1875 Aged 27 days
M. Grant (Lot 141), 1872–1930
Phoebe Cornelia (Lot 141), wife of S.M., b. May 12, 1833; d. Nov. 23, 1900
Sylvester M. (Lot 141), Veteran, d. Feb. 1, 1895; aged 69 yrs. 10 mos., 19 days
Thos. Lloyd (Lot 141) son of S.M. & C., d. Oct. 10, 1871; aged 2 mos., 18 days

BENNETT, Alvin S. (Lot 132), 1895–1980
Amelia Irene (Lot 132), wife of Martin A., 1858–1927
Geo. A. (Lot 132), d. Dec. 17, 1923; Aged 2 days
Lillian E. (Lot 132), 1913–
Martin A. (Lot 132), 1858–1929
Mattie Irean (Lot 132), daug. of M.A. & A.R., b. Aug. 3, 1891; d. Mar 24, 1903; "Our loved one," "Dearest daughter thou hast left us and our loss we deeply feel. But tis God that has bereft us. He can all our sorrows heal. Yet again we hope to meet thee when the day of life has fled and in heaven with joy to greet thee where no farewell tear is shed."

BLOCK, Berendje (Lot 85), 1865–1931
Reemt E. (Lot 85), 1867–1942

BOHNER George (Lot 148), 1868–1952
Marie (Lot 148), 1879–1951

BOOMBARDEN, Erna (Lot 116), 1893–1946
Herman (Lot 116) 1886–1980

BORCHERS, Betty (Lot 54), daug. of C. & J., d. July 20, 1871; Aged 9 yrs., 8 mos., 11 days; "Our Betty"
Carl (Lot 54), father, b. Sept. 29, 1814; d. Dec. 9, 1909
Jane (Lot 54), mother, wife of Carl, b. Mar. 28, 1824; d. Aug. 4, 1907
Morris H. (Lot 54), 1862–1918

BRADEN, John (Lot 41), Lieut. Co. C 11th Reg. Ia. Vol. Wounded near Leasburg Sept. 29 and died at Rolla Mo., C.W., d. Oct. 31, 1864; Aged 35 yrs., 2 mos.; "My husband"

BROCKA, Andrew P. (Lot 58), 1899–1969
Annie (Lot 64), 1887–1985
Chris Earl (Lot 64), IA. Sgt. 113 Calvary Recon sq. WWII, b. Aug. 27, 1917; d. Oct. 9, 1951; PH & OLC
Daughter (Lot 64), child of H.E.& Pearl, b. Nov. 3, 1927; d. Dec. 27, 1927
Edd (Lot 63)
Ernest (Lot 55), father, 1858–1923
Ernest C.A. (Lot 56), b. Mar. 22, 1911; d. Feb. 28, 1913; "We miss the voice of one we love. A precious form has passed away, to join the angel throng above in realms of endless day."
Genevieve L. (Lot 58), wife of Andrew, 1906–
Harry T. (Lot 55), son, 1905–1936
Harvey (Lot 64), 1900–1938
Ila Faye (Lot 63), 1933–1935
Mary H. (Lot 56), 1886–1975
Otto G. (Lot 56), 1887–1962
Robert David (Lot 64), infant son of H. & P., 1934
Susan (Lot 55), b. Oct. 24, 1897; d. Dec. 23, 1909; Aged 12 yrs., 1 mo., 29 days; "Gone but not forgotten"
Susan P. (Lot 55), mother, 1861–1951
Willie J. (Lot 64), 1885–1978

BUTLER, Birtha B. (Lot 10), daug. of P. & H.E.

BUTTON, E.D. (Lot 52), d. Mar. 1877; Aged 70 yrs., 6 mos.; "Good by, Gone but not forgotten"
CHAPMAN, Clarinda (Lot 49), mother, wife of Elisha, d. Oct. 7, 1877; Aged 61 yrs., 10 mos., 1 day; "Our mother"
Elisha (Lot 49)

CONN, Mary Ellen (Lot 7), daug. of Adam T. and Sarah Jane, b. March 10, 1855; d. Sept. 15, 1856

CRAIG, Alice E. (Lot 40), d. Aug. 28, 1875; Aged 11 mos., 24 days; "Sleep on sweet child and take thy rest. Earth's pangs with thee are o'er. The Savior took thee to his breast. Rest, Rest, thee ever more."
Geo. (Lot 40)
F. Melissa (Lot 40), wife of G.M., d. Nov. 19, 1878; Aged 30 yrs., 3 mos., 19 days
Georgie C. (Lot 40), d. Aug. 26, 1875; Aged 3 yrs., 2 mos., 8 days; "A father's hope—a mother's joy were centered in our only boy. Though of earthly hopes bereft yet one hope of heaven in left"

CRANDELL, Charley (Lot 9); "We miss thee Charley of how much. Sleep oh dear one and take thy rest. God called thee home, He thought it best."
John W. (Lot 9), son of C.N. & M.E., d. Nov. 27, 1888; Aged 20 yrs.

CUTSHALL, David W. (Lot 33), 1956–1966
Leo (Lot 33)

CUVALIER, Infant (Lot 5)
Mr. & Mrs. Virgil (Lot 5)

DAMHUIS, Peter (Lot 94), 1862–1953
Rosina (Lot 94), 1864–1932

DAVIS, (Lot 110S)
Everett L. (Lot 110S), son of J.W. & M.N., b. June 24, 1874; d. Sept. 9, 1874

DEBOER, Gertji Wissmann (Lot 133), 1861–1936

DEBOWER, Albert (Lot 138)
Clifton O. (Lot 7), b. Feb 19, 1926; d. May 8
Evelyn E. (Lot 93N), mother of Larry & Gary, wife of Louis, 1924–
Louis R. (Lot 93N), father of Larry & Gary, 1924–
Otto H. (Lot 7), 1888–1963
Rosa K. (Lot 7), 1889–1963

DEBUHR, Altje Janssen (Lot 99), wife of S.M., b. Sept. 6, 1848; d. Jan. 3, 1891
Bertha CH Lange (Lot 99), wife of S.M., b. July 16, 1849; d. Aug. 3, 1908
Dirk S. (Lot 7), father, b. Aug. 9, 1839; d. Dec. 23, 1914
E. Caroline S. (Lot 7), mother, b. Oct. 10, 1851; d. Feb. 7, 1928
Suntke M. (Lot 99), b. May 6, 1845; d. Nov. 4, 1922

DETTMERS, Dettmer (Lot 130-S1/2)
Geska Edeus, wife of D.
Dettmers—unmarked graves. Parents of, Kate (Mrs. Folkert Leerhoff), Mary (Mrs. C.H. "Charlie" Jacobs), & Henry Dettmers

DUNSON, Preston E. (Lot 101S), 1826–1912
Rebeca A. (Lot 101S), mother, wife of P.E., d. Feb. 3, 1890; Aged 61 yrs., 9 mos., 6 days; "Precious one from us has gone. A voice we love is stilled. A place is vacant in our home which never can be filled."

EGABROD, William Jasper (Lot 136S), son of Charles, d. July 25, 1911
Charles (Lot 136S)

ELLIOTT, Addie May (Lot 70W), daug. of F. & M.J., d. Sept. 29, 1874; Aged 1 yr., 7 mos., 20 days
Eddie (Lot 67), infant son of M. & M.E., d. Feb. 16, 1888; Aged 1 mo., 5 days

ELLIOTT, George (Lot 53), son of S. & L.J., d. Apr. 17, 1877
H. (Lot 01), b. May 25, 1822; d. Mar. 19, 1879
Levi (Lot 101N), Crpl. Co. G. 75 Ill Infantry, C.W., 1845–1908
Mary (Lot 67), infant daug. of M. & M.E., d. Dec. 29, 1878; Aged 27 days
Samantha J. (Lot 101N), mother, wife of Levi , d. June 7, 1890; aged 37 yrs., 6 mos., 12 days; "As a wife affectionate, as a mother devoted, as a friend ever kind and true"
Susan (Lot 70W), wife of Benjamin, d. Aug. 12, 1879; Aged 37 yrs., 4 mos., 14 days

ENDELMAN, Charles H. (Lot 145), father, 1886–1946
Dena (Lot 70), daug. 1900–1909
Flora (Lot 70), mother, 1862–1944
Harry (Lot 70), father, 1863–1946
Harry (Lot 145), son, d. Feb. 1914
Henry (Lot 70), son, 1890–1919
Infant (Lot 70), son, d. 1887
Martha B.M. (Lot 145), mother, 1890–1937

FELLOWS, (Lot 21)

FLESHNER, Anna T. Kramer (Lot 117), mother, b. Nov. 15, 1894; d. Mar. 1, 1986

FLITCRAFT, (Lot 48)

FREESE, Almuth (Lot 113), wife of F., b. Jan. 28, 1855; d. Dec. 30, 1898; "Rest in peace"
Andrew (Lot 37), father, b. May 18, 1851; d. Mar. 22, 1916
Andrew (Lot 128), 1893–1951

Baby (Lot 113), son of F. & A.

Eda (Lot 37), daug of A. & G., b. Aug. 30, 1888; d. Mar. 14, 1955

Gesina (Lot 37), wife of A., mother, b. Nov. 15, 1857; d. Mar. 28, 1903

Henry (Lot 128, 113)

Infant (Lot 37), son of A. & G., b. July 7, 1897; d. July 7, 1897

Martha (Lot 128), 1901–1968

Meint Wilhelm (Lot 113), son, b. Feb. 19, 1885; d. Nov. 15, 1911

Nettie (Lot 37), daug. of A. & G., b. Aug. 4, 1901; d. Feb. 12, 1902

FREESER, Grace (Lot 11), wife of Wesley, b. Apr. 6, 1836; d. Oct. 15, 1891; "At rest"

FREEZ, Wessel (Lot 11), b. Dec. 1832; d. Aug. 15, 1913

FREICHS, Baby (Lot 134), daug. of Pete & Gail, 1907

FRERICHS, Annie H. (Lot 98), 1869–1956

Enno H. (Lot 98), 1865–1944

Enno H. Jr. (Lot 98), son of Annie & Enno H., b. Mar. 29, 1908; d. Jan. 17, 1942

John (Lot 98), b. Dec. 25, 1905; d. Nov. 6, 1977

John (Lot 66)

Mattina, Trintje, b. Jan. 26, 1908; d. Mar. 11, 1908 (Lot 66)

Melvin George b. Oct. 21, 1906; d; Feb.1, 1908; "Budded on earth to bloom in Heaven" (Lot 66)

FRERICKS, Aletha (Lot 169), wife of Lindy, daug. of Dan Ganoung & Alma Carpenter, mother of Wylone Warring, 1920

Bilda (Lot 39), 1857–1935

George W. (Lot 83S), 1924–1970

Henry (Lot 39), 1852–1939

Jennie (Lot 39), 1901–1962

Leroy (Lot 39), b. Aug. 7, 1932; d. Feb. 5, 1933

Lindy D. (Lot 169), son of Matt Wolters & Jennie Frericks, 1927–

Margy E. (Lot 83S), 1927–

Matt (Lot 39), 1888–1953

FULS, Clarence (Lot 86), 1932–1934

Cornelius (Lot 86), 1904–1981

Grace H. (Lot 86), 1901–1976

GEER, Ed (Lot 82)

GONSALES, (Lot 23)

GRIPPEN, Laura (Lot 42NW), wife of Jas., born in Oswego Co. NY, d. Oct. 29, 1881; Aged 61yrs., 3 mos., 26 days

GROENEWOLD, Jan H. (Lot 114), son of J & M. b. Dec. 31, 1905; d. Aug. 8, 1908
John H. (Lot 114), b. Mar. 25, 1873; d. Feb. 10, 1910

HARTEMA , Baby (Lot 5)

HEEREN, Annette (Lot 79), wife of J., b. Apr. 12, 1873; d. Nov. 14, 1916
Eilt R. (Lot 69N), 1907–1982
Ella (Lot 80) 1890–1969
Flora G. (Lot 69N), 1909–1964
Harm C. (Lot 79), b. May 31, 1819; d. June 3, 1903
Heero A. (Lot 143) 1862–1943
Herman A. (Lot 80) 1893–1977
Infant (Lot 79) child of J. & A.
Infant (Lot 80), son of J. & E. 1930
Infant (Lot 69N), son of Eilt R., & Flora G., 1937
Jacob (Lot 79), 1864–1945
John E. (Lot 80), 1898–1983
Louise W., (Lot 143), 1872-1964 T.M., (Lot 79), wife of H.C.
Heeren, b. Sept. 4, 1821; d. Mar. 22, 1888

HENDRIX, Mary (Lot 22), daug. of N.B. & C.E., d. July 19, 1872; Aged 2 yrs., 6 mos.,
    17 days
Nels (Lot 22)

HENNING, Johann T. (Lot 114), 1871–1951
Marie H. (Lot 114), 1881–1966

HENRICHS, Delma E. (Lot 57), mother of Harley, Roger, Donald; 1913–
H. (Lot 50S), father, b. May 1, 1836; d. Aug. 21, 1916
Harm (Lot 20)
Henry S. (Lot 57), father of Harley, Roger, Donald; 1912–
Roger Dean (Lot 57), infant of H. & D., 1946

HESS, Dennis (Lot 148N)
Roberta Bohner (Lot 148N), mother of Dennis, James, Larry, Roger; 1921–1972

HINDERS, Annie (Lot 18), 1894–1918
Charlie (Lot 27)
Pete (Lot 18)
Shirley Ann (Lot 27), daug. of Charlie & Marie, b. Feb. 24; d. May 5, 1947

HINDIRS, Jessie Ruth (Lot 18), wife of Peter, b. in Germany, Nov. 22, 1860; d. Mar.
    27, 1911; "Rest darling rest"

HINRICHS, Anna (Lot 125), mother, wife of Siebelt, b. Jan. 15, 1850; d. June 28, 1946; "Rest in peace"

Entje K. (Lot 51S) 1871–1936

Flora (Lot 125), b. Dec. 23, 1870; d. Nov. 15, 1939; "Rest in peace"

Geo. (Lot 50N)

Gerd (Lot 50N), b. 1871; d. Mar. 24 1899: Aged 27 yrs., 3 mos., 29 days

Harm S. (Lot 124S) 1877–1969

Hinrich (Lot 50S), father, b. May 1, 1836; d. Aug. 21, 1918

Hinrich C. (Lot 20), b. June 2, 1856; d. Feb. 7, 1885

Jennie (Lot 124S), mother, 1877–1943

Johanna E. (Lot 125), b. Feb. 14, 1888; d. Jan. 29, 1920; "Rest in peace"

John G. (Lot 51S), father, 1864–1953

Maria (Lot 50S), mother, b. May 10, 1837; d. Apr. 9, 1926; "Rest in God"

Martta G. (Lot 20). d. Mar. 4, 1890

Siebelt (Lot 125), father, b. Aug. 24, 1844; d. June 27, 1920; "Rest in peace"

HOODJER, Anna (Lot 147), 1884–1981

Carl A. (Lot 144), Private, Buried in Manila, WWII, 1916–1942

Dena C. (Lot 144), mother, 1873–1949

John C. (Lot 144), father, 1872–1940

Philip C. (Lot 147), 1885–1921

Siebert G. (Lot 144), son of J.C. & D.C., 1910–1913

HOVENGA, Klopman (Lot 131)

HULSING, Annie Hinders (Lot 18), daug. of Peter & Geske Hinders, wife of John Hulsing, b. Sept. 27, 1894; d. May 4, 1918; Aged 23 yrs., 7 mos., 7 days; (name on stone misspelled Husling)

HUNTER, Allen (Lot 102) b Aug 2, 1856; d. Mar. 27, 1916

Alma E. (Lot 102), b. Mar. 7, 1858 d. May 4, 1927

Blanche (Lot 102), 1887–1970

Caroline (Lot 103), mother, wife of James, d. Sept. 16, 1886; Aged 55 yrs., 7 mos., 2 days; "At rest"

Elizabeth (Lot 103), d. Oct. 19, 1863; Aged 2 yrs., 9 mos.; "One less to love on earth, one more to meet in heaven"

James (Lot 103), father, d. Apr. 7, 1888; Aged 70 yrs., 11 mos., 2 days; "At rest"

Dr. James E. (Lot 103), son of James & Caroline, b. Oct. 9, 1867; d. June 18, 1897

Maud (Lot 102), daug. of A. & A.E., d. Sept. 28, 1886; Aged 1 yr., 10 mos., 4 days; "He shall gather the lambs with his arm and carry them in his bosom"

HUSLING, (Lot 18)

HYDE, Hanna (Lot 77), wife of Albert, b. Sept. 10, 1812, d. Feb. 25, 1890

Albert (Lot 77), b. Dec. 25, 1800; d. Sept. 10, 1886

JACOBS, Baby (Lot 146), child of J & T Jacobs, b. Jan. 20, 1908; d. Jan. 30, 1908
C.H. (Lot 127), father, b. Oct. 13, 1873; d. July 8, 1943
Charles Jr. (Lot 127), 1908–1912
Charlie (Lot 127), 1903–1978
Johann (Lot 146), b. May 14, 1878; d. Dec. 16, 1916
John (Lot 146)
John J. (Lot 62S), father of Eugene, RaDean; b. Jan. 31, 1917; d. Oct. 4, 1986
Kenneth (Lot 127), 1923–1958
Martha (Lot 62S), mother of Eugene, RaDean; 1919–1978
Mary (Lot 127), mother, b. Oct. 7, 1876; d. Aug. 6, 1936
Tena (Lot 146), b. Oct. 1, 1880; d. May 9, 1959
William H. (Lot 146), Minnesota Private. 34 Engrs., d. June 14, 1938

JANSSEN, Addo E. (Lot 124N), father of Robert, Ardis; 1900–1977
Anna H. (Lot 124N), mother of Robert, Ardis; 1909–
Robert H. (Lot 123)
Mrs. Robert H. (Lot 123)

JOHNSON, Alfred (Lot 4S)
Andrew H. (Lot 93S), father of Judith, Clifton, Margaret, Karen; 1917–
Charles Edward (Lot 63), son of Neva & George, d. Apr. 8, 1955
Edd H. (Lot 6), father, b. Sept. 6, 1887; d. June 10, 1958

JOHNSON, Elsena Rose (Lot 6), daug. of Ed & Rose; b. Apr. 3, 1916; d. May 2, 1916
Gerd (Lot 25), d. Mar. 18, 1895; Aged 44 yrs., 4 mos., 4 days
John F. (Lot 26), 1849–1937
Kathrine (Lot 26), 1855–1925
Rose A. (Lot 6), mother, b. Jan. 4, 1890; d. Apr. 22, 1977
Ruth M. (Lot 93S), mother of Judith, Clifton, Margaret, Karen; 1921–

JURGENS, Anna C. (Lot 36), wife of T., mother, b. Nov. 9, 1853; d. July 26, 1924
Audrey D. (Lot 4N), wife of Ted, 1922
Tamma C. (Lot 36), father, b. Apr. 19, 1847; d. Jan. 22, 1917
Ted M. (Lot 4N), 1919–1985

KINCADE, Addie (Lot 81), wife of Wm., d. Nov. 25, 1979; Aged 21 yrs., 4 mos., 19
    days; "And whither I go ye know, and the way ye know"

KLOPMAN or KOPEMANS (Lot 131)

KRAMER, Alfred H. (Lot 112), b. Feb. 11 1922; d. Apr. 8, 1931
Chriss S. (Lot 117), father, b. Oct. 20, 1896; d. Aug. 3, 1928; "Gone but not forgotten"
Fred W. (Lot 111 & 112), b. Feb. 13, 1875; d. Oct. 8, 1962
Frieda H. (Lot 112), b. Aug. 12, 1889; d. May 12, 1960
Mrs. Chriss S. (Lot 117), see Fleshner, Anna T. Kramer

Cemetery Records

KRULL, Heilkelina (Lot 95), wife of John, b. May 24, 1882; d. June 16, 1920
John (Lot 15), b. Jan. 14, 1877; d. Nov. 22. 1948
Rudolph (Lot 95), 1915–1986

LANDERS, Infants (Lot 56), twin daugs. of Galen & Marvel d. Aug. 19, 1949

LANPHIER, Adelia (Lot 140S), daug. of Isaac & Nancy, d. Dec. 31, 1869; Aged 13 yrs., 5 mos., 26 days; "Short was her stay in this vain world but long will be her rest: God took her home to dwell with him because he thought it best"
Issac (Lot 140S)

LATHROP, (Lot 77)
Eliza L. (Lot 110N), b. in Bozrah, CT., Nov. 7, 1832; d. July 27, 1878
Nellie Hyde (Lot 77), daug. of W.A. & A.A., d. Apr. 26, 1864; Aged 11 mos.

LAWRENCE, Elisabeth (Lot 140N) wife of R., d. Dec. 29, 1871 Aged 19 yrs., 9 mos.; "Dearest Elisabeth, thou art sleeping while thy mourners weep around. Thou waitest in thy grave to hear the trumpets joyful sound"
R. (Lot 140N)

LEERHOFF C. (Lot 129)
Clarence (Clarency) (Lot 19), 1905–1909
Edna (Lot 19), daug. of Folkert & Kate, d. 1908; Aged 8 mos.
Folke F. (Lot 19), mother, b. June 2, 1841; d. Apr. 19, 1905
Folkert (Lot 129), 1872–1909
Henry (Lot 129), 1903–1927
Jurke (Lot 20), wife of R., b. Mar. 25, 1847; d. Feb. 7, 1889
Kate (Lot 129), wife of F., 1872–1909
Rickelt (Lot 19), husband of Jurke
Sieger H. (Lot 19), father, b. 25, Apr. 1841 in Engerhafe kreis Aurieh, Ostfriesland; d. 25 June 1899

LIENEMANN, Lubbo (Lot 116), father, 1860–1933
Luise Kannegiesser (Lot 116), wife of L., mother, b. June 14, 1872; d. June 23, 1915

LINDAMAN, Rick (Lot 43)

MARAGRETZ, Sarah (Lot 104), d. June 29, 1887; Aged 70 yrs., 9 mos., 12 days

MARGRETZ, Charles H. (Lot 104), son of H.H. & S.M., d. July 18, 1857; Aged 15 yrs., 9 Mos., 25 days.

MARTIN, (Lot 21)
George E. (Lot 69S)
Gracie (Lot 69S), daug. of Geo. E. & E., d. July 11, 1870; Aged 11 mos.
Jennie (Lot 69S), daug. of H.E. & G.E., d. Apr. 5, 1875

MAYER, Andrew (Lot 13), father, b. Sept. 25; 1877; d. Feb. 4, 1931
Clara D. (Lot 13), mother of James, Carole, Paul; 1910–
Friedrich H. (Lot 13), b. Feb. 12, 1915; d. Feb. 18, 1917; "Rest in peace"
George J. (Lot 13), father of James, Carole, Paul; 1907–1979
Rosina (Lot 13), mother, b. Sept. 29, 1878; d. Aug. 6, 1962

MEENTS, Jasine (Lot 143), 1868–1936

MERRILL, Rev. Richard (Lot 68), d. Dec. 4, 1875; Aged 62 yr.
William Howard (Lot 68), d. Sept. 3, 1865; Aged 1 yr., 7 Mos., 29 days.

MERRILLS, Nellie (Lot 42), daug. of G.E. & L., d. Sept. 1, 1880, Aged 1 yr., 10 mos.,
    4 days

MOORHEAD, Charlotte (Lot 72), daug. of J.G. & M.
John (Lot 72)
Martha (Lot 74), wife of R., d. Sept. 19, 1870; Aged 86 yr.

MOORHEAD, Robert, (Lot 74), d. May 31, 1871; Aged 91 yrs.

McELHANEY, Allie (Lot 38), son of J.R. & E.M., d. Apr. 10, 1877; Aged 2 yrs., 7
    mos., 12 days
Eda (Lot 38), daug. of J.R. & E.M., d. May 2, 1877; aged 6 yrs., 8 mos.

OLTMANN, Edward (Lot 62N), 1908–1973
Laura A. (Lot 62N), 1911–

OLTMANNS, Hilkea (Lot 130-N½), mother, 1850–1936
John (Lot 130N), father, 1852–1936
Reiner (Lot 130N), b. July 28, 1886; zu Jever Grossherz (ogtum) Oldenburg, d. May
    5, 1909

OSGOOD, (Lot 10)

PAGEL, Ferdinand E. (Lot 8), father, b. July 17, 1879; d. Sept. 24, 1955
Margaret (Lot 8), 1852–1929
Susie (Lot 8), mother, b. Apr. 10, 1885; d. Apr. 27, 1961
William (Lot 8), 1850–1929

PALMER, Francis (Lot 139), son of Jno. & P.R. d. Nov. 10, 1866; Aged 16 yrs., 3 mos.,
    3 days

RADEMAKER, Henry (Lot 83N)
REIHER, (Lot 10)
Henry (Lot 35), father, b. June 30, 1854; d. Apr. 3, 1919

Marie A. (Lot 35), b. Aug. 12, 1889; d. Sept. 4, 1977

Theresa (Lot 35), wife of Henry, mother, b. Dec. 12, 1856; d. Nov. 13, 1930

REINTS, Elsine C. (Lot 109), b. July 19, 1889; d. Dec. 21, 1890

Elsine BA (Lot 109), b. Feb. 1, 1892; d. Apr. 19, 1892

Elso (Lot 109), b. Mar. 11, 1887; d. Dec. 20, 1900

Elzina Groeneveld (Lot 142), wife of G.A., mother, b. Aug. 22, 1846; d. Sept. 8, 1931

Emilie H. (Lot 24), b. Jan. 5, 1893; d. May 21, 1960

Frank G. (Lot 24), b. July 24, 1882; d. June 23, 1972; "I know that my redeemer lives"

George G. (Lot 142)

Gerhard (Lot 109)

Gerhard A. (Lot 109), b. Nov. 21, 1881; d. Dec. 22, 1900

Gerhard Albertus (Lot 142), father, b. Feb. 21, 1847; d. Oct. 4, 1911

Helen E. (Lot 24), b. Aug. 5, 1923

Hinrich F.G. (Lot 109), b. Nov. 12, 1874; d. Nov. 20, 1902

Infant (Lot 142), son of F.G. & E.H. d. Jan. 25, 1919

Johann (Lot 109), b. Mar. 28, 1878; d. Dec. 20, 1900

Ontje (Lot 109), b. June 29, 1888; d. Sept. 6, 1888

Wea Sissingh (Lot 142), wife of Johann, b. Sept. 13, 1848 in Osfriesland, d. Apr. 7, 1927 in Waterloo, IA.

RESSLER, Hettie S. (Lot 104), daug. of A.R. & A.R., d. Sept. 5, 1860; Aged 1 yr., 11 mos., 15 days

Hubert W. (Lot 84), 1899–1941

Infant (Lot 84), daug. of H.W. & S.C. 1922

John H. (Lot 104), son of A.R. & A.R., d. Sept. 21, 1960; Aged 4 yrs., 3 days

Mary Jean (Lot 84), b. Mar. 21, 1931; d. May 18, 1933

RUEHAAK, A. Henry (Lot 94), 1885–1964

Anna L. (Lot 94), 1885–1947

RYAN, Henry F. (Lot 136S), 1884–1967

SANTEE, Carrie M. (Lot 108), b. Mar. 11, 1869; d. Sept. 20, 1886

Fredrick E. (Lot 108), b. Oct. 9, 1852; d. Aug. 27, 1856

Harry (Lot 108), b. May 30, 1859; d. Oct. 8, 1859

Joseph (Lot 108)

SCHRAGE, Abel (Lot 126), b. Feb. 15, 1912; d. June 3, 1912

Freeda (Lot 126), 1884–1972

Joe (Lot 126), 1876–1956

SHAFFER, Adam (Lot 97)

SIEFKES, Alina W. (Lot 34), b. Oct. 24, 1845; d. Dec. 17, 1918; "Here rest in Christ"
Alina Wilhemine Emilie (Lot 34), b. Mar. 30, 1891; d. May 29, 1896
Augusta (Lot 34), b. Jan. 23, 1874; d. Feb. 23, 1962; "The Lord is my light and my salvation" Ps. 27:1
Elizabeth (Lot 34), b. Feb. 4 1870; d. Mar. 26, 1922; "Hold me not up for the Lord has given me Grace for my journey. Let me go to my Lord"
S.H. (Lot 34), Pastor, b; May 26, 1866; d. Nov. 5, 1947; "He consumed himself to give light to others"

STOPPELMOOR, Babe (Lot 115)
Harm (Lot 96), 1910–
Mary (Lot 96), 1866–1948
Mary (Lot 96S), 1888–1976
Mary Alice Bingham (Lot 115), mother, wife of Rudolf, b. June 14, 1901; d. Apr. 8, 1926
Mattie (Lot 96), 1907–1977
Minnie (Lot 96), 1901–
Rudolf (Lot 115), father, 1887–1972
Si L (Lot 96), 1861–1939
Walter (Lot 96), California, PFC HQ 389 Mil Police Bn WWII, b. Dec. 3, 1906; d. Oct. 29, 1960

STUART, Elizabeth Jane (Lot 107) daug. of Charles & Margaret, b. Jan. 1855; d. Aug. 28, 1856
John (Lot 107), son of Charles & Margaret, b. April 1853; d. Sept. 3, 1856

TAYLOR, Elizabeth (Lot 72), d. Nov. 2, 1867; Aged 87 yrs.
(Lot 72), d. Sept. 19, 1869; Aged 51 yrs.

VAN LENGEN, Ben (Lot 3)
Beverly Sue (Lot 8), infant, d. Oct. 17, 1952

VOIGTS, Emma D. (Lot 71), daug. of H. & J., 1859–1869
Henry (Lot 71), 1813–1908
Johanna (Lot 71), 1824–1896
Marie S. (Lot 71), daug. of H. & J., 1853–1869

WALKER, Harrie Marshall (Lot 137), infant son of H.N. & C.A., d. July 8, 1873; Aged 8 mos., 8 days; "Only waiting"

WERKMAN, Trenje (Lot 75), wife of Engel, b. June 13, 1905; age 28 yrs; "Rest in peace"

WILDEBOER, Amanda (Lot 28), 1915–1918
Bruno (Lot 65), b. Sept. 22, 1894; d. Dec. 5, 1911; "Rest in peace"

Casjen A. (Lot 28), 1915–
Florence L. (Lot 65), mother, 1893–1928
Foalka (Lot 65), 1855–1943
Phillip (Lot 65), 1854–1932

WILFON, Harold (Lot 83N), Buried in unmarked grave. Passing through the area, he had stayed to work for Henry Rademaker. He was said to be from Germany and died ca. 1910–1912 in his fifties.

WISSMAN, Anna (Lot 133), 1902–1903
J. (Lot 133)

WITHERS, Bertha Wolford (Lot 12), daug. of John & Laura Wolford, b. Mar. 9, 1902; d. Jan. 29, 1972

WOLFORD, Birdie May (Lot 12), daug. of John & Laura, b. Mar. 9, 1902; d. Apr. 26, 1902
John (Lot 12)

WOLTERS, Annie (Lot 100), 1874–1958
Dorothy (Lot 51N), wife of Henry, 1909–1935
George (Lot 100), 1867–1931
Henry (lot 51N), 1895–1981
Hilka (Lot 100), 1917–1948
Jennie (Lot 51N), wife of Henry, 1883–1954
John (Lot 166)
Mrs. G. (Lot 100)
Otto (Lot 100), 1898–1984
Reiner (Lot 100), 1896–1975

WUST, Bernadine (Lot 05), mother of Berdine, Amelia, Margaret, Raymond; 1899–1979
Eileen A. (Lot 87), mother of Michael, Darlys, Mishelle, Kathleen, Rebecca, Mark; 1933–
Infant (Lot 85), son of Mr. Mrs. R., d. Oct. 1, 1923; Body buried in N.J.
Margaret (Lot 85), b. Jan. 25, 1927; d. Feb. 1, 1927
Raymond (Lot 87), father of Michael, Darlys, Mishelle, Kathleen, Rebecca, Mark; 1930–
Reinhold (Lot 85), father of Berdine, Amelia, Margaret, Raymond; 1890–1971

YOST, Jacob (Lot 78)
Lucretia A. (Lot 78), daug. of Jacob & Evalina, d. Oct. 1, 1864; Aged 5 yrs., 2 mos., 10 days; "Sleep dear child and be at rest. Thy spirit dwells among the blest"

Additions

FRERICHS, Anna Leona daug of John and Tena Heitland Frerichs Jan 26, 1913–1914
Lester Lyle son of John and Tena Heitland Frerichs
(missing lamb stone) Oct 28, 1918 Apr 11, 1920
Two Frerichs Babies d July 21, 1921 d Aug 18, 1921
One stillborn Baby no

Butler Center Veterans

Elliot, Levi...Civil War
Broden, John...Civil War
Bailey, Martin...Civil War
Jacobs, Will... World War I
Stopplemore, Rudolph...World War I
Baldwin, Sylvestor...World War I
Hoodjer, Carl...World War II
Brocke, Chris...World War II
Stopplemore, Walter...World War II
Jacobs, John...World War II

Death in Allison

We have occasion this week to chronicle the first death that has ever occurred in Allison. It was mentioned last week that the little child of Mr. and Mrs. Geo. M. Craig was dangerously sick and the little one continued to grow worse until Tuesday night, when the little spirit was wafted heavenward leaving the fond parents to mourn the loss of that which was near and dear to them. The funeral took place at the residence yesterday afternoon at 3 o'clock, and the remains were taken to Butler Center for interment.

The bereaved parents have the heartfelt sympathy of the entire community in their affliction.
—Allison Tribune, *August 18, 1881*

BEAVER GROVE CEMETERY

Beaver Grove Cemetery is located in Section 20, Beaver Township, about three miles northwest of New Hartford. It was organized on March 19, 1882, at a meeting held in the District 1 schoolhouse. Noah Bowen donated the ground, providing the association kept up the fences. Trees were cleared off, and lots of six spaces were sold for five dollars each.

Past presidents of the association have been Nate Olmstead, Noah Bowen, Ira Ingalls, T.G. Olmstead, G.B. Luck, Mrs. Anna Ingalls, Pearl Ingalls, Mrs. Dick Thomas, Cena Ackerson and Clyde Garner, who served in the office for thirty-four years (1930–64). Present officers are Martin Holm, president, and Mrs. Harold Chapman, secretary.

Veterans Buried in Beaver Grove Cemetery

Civil War
Belt, A.J.
Bowen, Noah
Clayton, Dow
Farnswroth, L.H.
Higgins, H.H.
Lee, Major William
Mead, Philo
Olmstead, Rev. Nathan
Thomas, Henry
Unknown soldier

Mexican
Beckwith, Royce

World War I
Evers, Treno
Luck, Ernest
Luck, Orion
McCoun, Art
Smith, George
Way, Ross

World War II
Boltz, Elmer F.
Brennan, William G.
Luck, Eugene
Nielsen, Darrel
Geyer, Chris A.

Burials

Ackerson, Mrs. Isaac No dates 5/77
Ackerson, Will W. Our darling aged ld June 19, 1879 2/56

Beckwith, Royce Co. E 2nd Reg T Iowa Vol Inf Mexican War 4/76
Belfield, Leslie C. 1910–1985 8/26
Belt, A.J. Co. E 44 Iowa Infantry CW Vet No dates 5/23
Bolton, Cecil A. 189?–1958 7/61
Bolton, Flora L. Feb 24, 1889 Aged 26ylm2d 5/59
Boltz, Elmer F. 1927–1984 Tec 5 US Army WWII Jan 15, 1927–June 17, 1984 5/68
Boltz, Sarah M. 1929–   parents of Linda 5/68
Bowen, Charles No dates 6/67
Bowen, Eliza No dates 6/67
Bowen, Noah 1835–1916 CW Vet 4/69
Bowen, Cynthia 1835–1912 4/69
Bowen, Hadassah wife of W. 83y 1881 4/69
Bowen, Paul Wesley 1912 s of M.A. 2/38
Brennan, Willie 1881–1953 3/21
Brennan, Grace Luck 1880–1969 3/21
Brennan, William WWII 1913–1956 Private.
Brennan, Wm. G. Co B 1284th Eng. Combat Battalion 3/21
Brennan, Lot bought 1897 No dates 8/80
Brennan, Fred 8/80
Brennan, Lucille 8/80
Brennan, John 8/80

Clayton, Dow Mar 14, 1833-Jun 27, 1893 60y 3m 13d CW 4/76

DeBuhr, John 1899–1984 7/66B
DeBuhr, Ethel 1900–1972 parents of Eva, Nettie, Dorothy & John Jr. 7/66B
DeBuhr, Nan 1903–1982 8/26
DeBuhr, Verda 1911–   8/26

Ehling, Children of C.M. 3/75
Ehling, Darcy Dec 19, 1879–Aug 21, 1886 3/75
Ehling, Wilhemenia Feb 1, 1890–Feb 10, 1890 3/75
Ehling, Wilhelm May 22, 1893–Jun 5, 1893 3/75
Ehling, Elizabeth Nov 14, 1883–Aug 27, 1891 3/75
Evers, Treno J. 1895–1964 WWI 8/62
Evers, Jennie wife of Treno 1902–1949 8/62
Evers, John 1920–1938 8/62
Evers, Clarence 1922–1940 8/62

Farnswroth, L.M. Civil War Co. H 16th Wis Inf No dates 6/24
Farnswroth, Eliza M. mo. 1857–1932 6/24
Farnswroth, Little Guy s of L.M.& E.M. d May 7,1881 8m 8d 6/31
Flynn, Grace Apr 23, 1887 9m daug of J.J. & Minnie nee Ingalls 2/71

Garner, Clyde 1886–1971 4/40
Garner, Eva 1885–1974 4/40
Garner, Jennie (no stone) 3/4a
Geyer, Chris 1868–1942 6/42
Grandon, Clyde 1910–   9/45
Grandon, Evelyn 1918–   9/45
Grandon, Nelson W. 1870–1938 8/65
Grandon, Erma S. 1878–1961 8/65
Grandon, Spencer E. 1907–1968 8/65
Grandon, Mabel 1911–   8/65
Grandon, William 1833–1897 3/52

Hattie, I. 1868–1951 6/42
Hattie, Carrie 1895–1973 6/42
Hattie, Chris A. 1901–1968 WWII 8/29B
Hattie, Marlys E. 1920–   8/29B
Heckenlively, Thelma Irene Feb. 22, 1913–Mar 2, 1986 5/5
Higgins, H.H. Government Scout No dates CW 4-69
Hinders, Fannie wife of Peter Sept 10, 1890 35y 8/8
Hoffman, Infant daug of H.A. & E.J. Nov 30, 1891 6/60
Holm, Betty 1931 sister 7/30
Holm, Francis 1934 brother 7/30
Holm, Hazel Leta No dates 6/60
Holm, Nartin P. No dates 6/60 (Martin?)
Hummel Wm. R. s of Roman & Minnie Geyer 1898–1976 6/42

Ingalls, Alice M. 1868–1925 3/57
Ingalls, Arthur W. 1863–1925 3/57
Ingalls, Archie Our darling baby s of A.W. & M. Jan 20, 1885 Aged 2m 28d 3/57
Ingalls, Lloyd 1894–1917 3/57
Ingalls, Donald E. 1919–1920 1/55
Ingalls, Evelyn P. 1921–1922 1/55
Ingalls, Ira W. 1837–1912 3/70
Ingalls, Baby 1886 3/70
Ingalls, Anna E. 1844–1919 3/70
Ingalls, Ira M. 1838–1912 3/70

Johnson, Katie No dates 6/67
Johnson, Tolif Apr 27, 1829–May 24, 1906 5/68
Johnson, Martha M. Oct 24, 1842–Nov 18, 1902 5/68

LeBahn, Adolph Dec 4, 1837–Feb 18, 1909 4/58
LeBahn, Louise July 31, 1839–Apr 20, 1900 4/58
LeBahn, Lloyd 1894–1917 4/58
Lee, Major William CW Vet
Lee, Unmarked grave 4/40
Luck, Clyde 1945–   1/1
Luck, Linda K. 1948–   parents of Clyde Jr. & Michele 1/1
Luck, Florence Mar 26, 1928–Sept 29, 1986 9/10
Luck, Ernest A. Jr. 1910–1977 4/3
Luck, Verbena E. 1916–   4/3
Luck, Ernest A. 1871–1936 5/6
Luck, Kenneth A. 1940–1941 5/6
Luck, Dorothy M. 1914–1957 5/6
Luck, Clifford F. 1905–1973 5/6
Luck, Lester D. 1931–1973 5/6
Luck, Eugene 1924–1979 WWII 2/2
Luck, Dorothy 1924–1975 parents of David & Dianne 2/2
Luck, Fred 1893–1982 1/72
Luck, Evelyn 1904–   1/72
Luck, George 1856–1921 2/20
Luck, Josephine wife of George 1854–1899 Aged 45y 6m 28d 2/20
Luck, Greenbury B. 1833–1925 4/33
Luck, Susan 1838–1920 4/33
Luck, George M. s of J.T. & S.M. d
Luck, Catherine July 22, 1859–Sept 7, 1871 4/33
Luck, Carrie Mar 30, 1872–Apr 23, 1913 4/33
Luck, Keitha Irene Nov 20, 1911 4/33
Luck, Haley June 11-17-1978 I pray the Lord my soul to keep 8/9
Luck, Harley 1934–1974 7/8
Luck, Thomas A. Aug 13, 1964–Apr 17, 1976 Our beloved son and brother
Luck, Herman 1899 3/4B
Luck, Wava 1906–   parents of James, Eunice, Lavern, Verna & Dale 3/4B
Luck, John T. 1864–1951 2/38
Luck, Sophia LeBahn May 1, 1867–Dec 21 1927 2/38
Luck, Ernest A. 1891–1952 WWI 2/38
Luck, John G. 1924–   1/4
Luck, Georgia L. 1927–   1/4
Luck, Orion 1896–1944 WWI Vet Post Commander Am Leg 2/17
Luck, Clara Johnson 1902–   m 1920 parents of John, Eugene, Maveleen
    2/17
Luck, Baby No dates 2/17
Luck, Raymond 1904–1957 1/18
Luck, Ruth J. 1910–1974 Am Leg Aux 1/18
Luck, Mary 1928 1/18

Luck, Lois 1930 1/18
Luck, Blanch 1933 1/18
Luck, Glee 1936 1/18
Luck, Si Feb 29, 1908–June 16, 1986 8/11
Luck, Bernice E. Mar 28, 1907–Mar 17, 1986 8/11

McCoun, Art 1889–1968 WWI 8/44
McCoun, Mattie 1903–1981 8/44
Mead, Philo C.W. Vet No dates 6/13B
Mead, Elva wife of Philo d Nov 22, 1873 Aged 21y7m 6/13B
Moon, Howard lot, cement slab but stone missing 8/47
Moon, Marilyn Dec 24, 1938 8/47
Moore, Earl D. 1880–1959 8/44
Moore, Mabel 1882–1973 8/44
Moore, George 1905– 9/28
Moore, Hilda 1917– 9/28
Moore, Peter 1947–1982 9/28
Munger, Charles A. Aug 28, 1873–Jan 2, 1957 1/37
Munger, Mary L. LeBahn Jan 8, 1874–Sept 17, 1929 1/37
Murray, Mrs. Ralph 1935–1959 8/29A
Murray, Vindetta 1867–1912 WRC 3/39
Murray, William C. 1862–1917 3/39

Nabor, George H. 1897–1964 9/46
Nabor, Amy D. 1912–1981 9/46
Nielsen, Darell WWII Unmarked grave 7/12

Olmstead, Aaron June 25, 1828–Feb 13, 1913 6/31
Olmstead, Hulda M. Jan 11, 1832–Sept 28, 1900 6/31
Olmstead, Isaac son of A. & H. d Oct 2, 1872 Aged 19 y lm 5d 6/31
Olmstead, Florence d Sep 21, 1872 Aged 1y 10 d daug of A.M. & H.M. 6/31
Olmstead, A.L. Nov 2, 1833–1919 5/41
Olmstead, Margaret wife of A.L. Aug 13, 1832–June 12, 1859 5/41
Olmstead, Mary Jane daug of A.L. & M. Jan 2, 1857–Mar 14, 1872 5/41
Olmstead, O.D. No dates 5/41
Olmstead, Fannie R. wife of O.D. Jan 4, 1867 Aged 23y 11 m 2d 5/41
Olmstead, Frank L. 1859–1955 2/35
Olmstead, Angeline 1870–1938 2/35
Olmstead, Archie 1887–1929 s. 2/35
Olmstead, Rev. Nathan d May 7, 1889 Aged 79y 7m 21d Vol Co E 32nd Ia Inf CW
    Vet 4/51B
Olmstead, Julia wife of Nathan d Mar 7, 1890 Aged 82 y 8m 3d 4/51 C
Olmstead, Little Willie son of T.G. & G. d 1869 Aged 40mos 4/51A
Olmstead, Sarah C. 1863–1952 6/42
Olmstead, Silas Eugene 1856–1928 6/42

Parsons, Emma L. mo. 1889–1938 7/48
Parsons, Wilbert E. f. 1879–1938 7/48
Parsons, Harold 1903–1937 1/19
Parsons, James f. 1857–1941 6/78
Parsons, Sarah A. mo. 1859–1937 6/78
Parsons, Grace daug of J.B. & S.A. Oct 8, 1887–June 12, 1890 6/78
Percy, Jane wife of M.M. Apr 29, 1834–Feb 3, 1916 5/50
Philo, Wm. Jan 7, 1847–Jan 13, 1868 5/50
Philo, Wm. M. 1802–July 22, 1868 Aged 66y 3m 20d 5/50
Philo, Lucinda wife of Wm. d. Dec 22, 1888 Aged 84y 9m 5d 5/50

Root, Mary E. wife of J.F. Mar 31, 1860 Aged 27y 4/22
Root, Ella d Mar 27 1864 4y 6m4 d Memory faithful to its trust Regails you in beauty
    from the dust 4/22

Schneiderman, Delbert T. 1912–1955 7/30
Schneiderman, Berneice 1912–   7/30
Sells, Iva M. 1872–1952 2/56B
Sells, Nathan G. 1870–1937 2/56B
Smith, George Allen 1897–1935 Private. 88 Infantry 19 Div WWI 1/36
Smith, Muriel 1901–1975 1/36
Smith, George L. son of L.L. & D. d Nov.8, 1865 Aged 2y 5/32
Smith, Julia E. d Apr 6, 1863 Aged 2y 6/32
Smith, Henry d May 28, 1963 Aged 5y 5/32
Smith, Thomas Dick D. 1877–1937 1/72
Smith, Pearl Ingalls 1874–1934 1/72
Smith, Baby Earl 1902 1/72
Smith, Henry Nov 29, 1829–Mar 4, 1863 d at Fort Pillow Tenn. CW Vet 6/49
Smith, Louisa M. Mar 2, 1830–Sept 9, 1896 6/49
Smith, Henry J. s of H. &L.M. Apr 28, 1863–Feb 8, 1864 6/49

Timmons, children of Ezra D. & C. 6/13A
Timmons, Tracy Aug 11, 1901–Aug 13, 1902 6/13A
Timmons, Infant Nov 4, 1900 6/13A
Tucker, Cornelia wife of Samuel d May 30, 1906 Aged 49y 3m 11d 4/15

Way, Ross Pf c Co D 408 Telegraph Bn. WWI Sept 4, 1886–July 1, 1961 5/14
Webster, Merilda mo. 1856–1891 2/74
Whipple, Perry M. d Aug 15, 1877 3m 11d 6/5
Whipple, Phillip Aged 10d 6/5
Whipple, Sarah R. d July 2, 1862 Aged 1y 5m 19d 6/5
Whipple, Nelson H. 1832–1907 6/5
Whipple, Zillah wife. No dates 6/5
Whipple, Nelson Adolph Dec 14, 1870–1942 6/5
Whipple, Whitney, Charles No dates 6/67
Whipple, Minnie No dates 6/67

THE COSTER CEMETERY

The Coster Cemetery is located in Section 22 of Jefferson Township, Butler County, Iowa. The land was originally owned by John Coster and was about a half mile from the Salem Evangelical Association Church. While the earliest readable date on a gravestone is 1871, county records state that on or about January 31, 1874, the above-named real estate was conveyed by John Coster and his wife to the trustees of Salem Evangelical Church. Some early county death records list place of burial as "German Church Cemetery" or "Salem Cemetery," and one reads "one-half mile south of the German church." There is also on file at the recorder's office a deed dated May 3, 1913. George Pohl, C.L. Renning and H.F. Renning, trustees of the Salem Evangelical Church, conveyed the property to the Coster Cemetery Association.

Across from the cemetery stands the foundation fragments of an early building of the once town of Coster. A lot number follows each name listed in the following pages.

A four-member board presently oversees the cemetery: Ernie Ramige, president; Faye Vossberg, secretary/treasurer; Jim Miller; and Louise Lalan. Ernie Ramige does the mowing, and Jim Miller digs the graves.

Burials are current only through 1999.

Coster Cemetery. *Taken by Shirley Miller, 2008, used with her permission.*

ADAMS, John K. Lot 48 10-31-1892 11-25-1922

BAUMAN, Helen Francis Lot 40 10-9-1913 4-16-1914
Hindertje 1876–1960 Lot 40
Diedrich Lot 40 1875–1960
John Lot 40 1911–1937

BRENNER, George Lot 29 8-6-1877–?

BUCHEISTER, John (No stone) Lot 21

BUSSE, Elmer Lot 63

COSTER, John B. Lct 7 3-4-1847–8-26-1924
Minnie (wife) Lot 7 1841–1920

DUKS, Herman (Infant) Lot 51 8-5-190?–10-11-190?

DRENTH, Ben Lot 48 9-11-1919–3-20-1920
Psalm 33:4 For the word of the Lord is right and all his works are done in Truth.

EARSEY, Mrs. Lot 54

FOLKEN, Nan Lot 43 11-1885–1943
Jennie Lot 43 1889–1969

FREELAND, Charley Lot 59 1876–1950
Julia (daug. E. Immery) Lot 59 1880–1970

GOODNACHT, Lewis Lot 23 11-14-1824–5-19-1914
Dora Lot 23 3-16-1821–5-10-1903

HAHN, Freddie Lot 42 9-22-1893–1898
George (son of George & Anna) Lot 42 6-7-1905–6-12-1905
Another child of George & Anna Lot 42 No dates
Marie Lot 24 8-20-1834–8-19-1887
Son of Ernest & Hilka Lot 50 5-12-1897–5-12-1897
Son of Ernest & Hilka Lot 50 2-14-1918–2-14-1918

HALL, Baby Lot 32 1 mo 12 day 1920

HARD (Hart), Daniel Lot 23 12-11-1850–2-28-1931
Louise Lot 23 6-14-1855–2-28-1931
Infant sons Lot 23 12-22-1874 6-4-1876 12-17-1879

HART, Aloysia Lot 36 1834–1926
Daniel Lot 36 1814–1884
Emma Lot 38 1856–1938
Ernest P. Lot 37 1881–1904
Eureka Lot 51 1857–1920
Frederich William Lot 37 1-7-1842–1-5-1920
Jennie Lot 37 4-4-1855–7-20-1946
Philip Lot 51 1848 No date cut
Steve Lot 25 6 graves
William F. Lot 37 6-4-1878–4-10-1880
William Lot 38 1853–1908
4 children Lot 38
Elnore B. Lot 56 1-9-1914–2-11-1914
3 sons of Aloysia & Daniel Lot 36

HINDERS, Kneal Lot 64 1889–1957
Minnie Lot 64 1892–1971

IMMING E. Lot 59 No dates

JANS, Minnie Ahlers Lot 47 1880–1974
Minnie (daug.) Lot 47 6-16-1919–3-20-1920
Wubbo Lot 47 1863–1937

JACOBS, Julius Lot 15 4-29-1873–9-3-1873

JAQUIS, Uns Lot 32 4-18-1888–12-24-1909

JONAS, Johann Lot 9 9-1813–9-1886
John (son) Lot 9 1-26-1865–10-12-1880
Sophie (wife) Lot 9 ?–1907
2 children (No marker)

JONES, Eddie Lot 28 (Son of William & Mary)
Ruth Lot 28 1894
Twin boys Lot 28 1896

KLUITER Baby of John & Grace Lot 39 No stone

KOEHN, Osoah Nathan (Son of Bert M. Koehn) Lot 29 9-23–1880 9yrs 5 mo 8 days

KRETSCHNER, Lois Lot 35 1861–1888
LANG, Paul Son of David & Eva Lot 29 12-3-1907–6-10-1908

LENNENBECK, Mother Lot 5 D 4-14-1875 73 yrs.

LUBBEN, Fenne Lot 20 1844–1904
Gerhard Lot 20 1848–1923

MEDDERS, Martha Lot 59 1899–1934

METHFESSEL, Father Lot 54 9-2-1834–11-24-1916
Mother Lot 54 7-5-1834–2-17-1906

MEYERS, Herrold Lot 10 9-15-1890–4-29-1902

MILLER, Catherine Lot 53 1846–1913
Stella Lot 53 1879–
Viola Lot 53 (daug. of A & G) D 3-27-1884 7 months

MODDERMAN, Elsie Lot 55 1916–1931

NATZKE, Anna Lot 30 D 7-19-1893 72 yrs old
August Lot 30 D 1-2-1890 69 yrs old
August Lot 30 (son of August & Anna) 5-22-1871

NEGAN, Fred Lot 55 (Son of Jake & Lena) 9-13-1910–1-28-1926
Henry Lot 55 2 yrs

PAGEL, Vern

POHL, Francis May Lot 46 (Daug. of George & Mena) 7-28-1890–9-6-1895

POPPEN, Alme Lot 19 1915–1935
Edna F. Lot 44 9-23-1894–10-11-1897
Harm Lot 19 9-19-1841–11-30-1905
Mable Marlys Lot 19
Rolfken G. Lot 19 1-10-1842–10-21-1910
Infant Son Lot 19 1930

PORMAN, John Lot 8 2-20-1827–3-10-1894 67 yr.
Minnie Lot 8 D 5-12-1900 62 yr.
Minnie Lot 8 (Daug. of John & Minnie) D 5-24-1889 20 yr 3 mo.

RAMIGE, Daug. of Don & Anna Lot 44 B & D 1943
Mary A. Lot 44 1880–1944
Newton S. Lot 44 1876–1937
REIHER, C.F. Lot 6 9-2-1880–5-2-1917
Emila (daug.) Lot 6 5-28-1863–1-21-1884
Mary (wife) Lot 6 9-6-1832–7-16-1904

RENNING, Camilla May Lot 43 (daug. of C.L. & M.A.) 8-21-1901–9-16-1904
Carl Lot 5 5-9-1831–12-18-1906
Christina Lot 5 6-2-1834–3-31-1923
Minnie A. Lot 26 3-11-1857–9-20-1894

RETTLEIN, Frau Anna Lot 34 6-1837–4-27-1903
Baby Lot 34 1903

SCHONEMAN, John Lot 40 1889–1956
Kate Lot 40 1896–1949

SELIGER, Alice Mary Lot 36 1912–1923
Florence Lot 36 1923 No marker

SCHILLING, Sophie Tackman Lot 4 10-28-1856–9-19-1943

SHORTER, James Lot 33 (Son of W & E) 7-29-1877 1 yr. 4 mo. 3 days

TACHMAN, Henry Lot 4 11-28-1857–10-24-1902

TIMER, George Lot 60 1919–1927
George (son of Steffen & Flora) Lot 60 3-3-1908–5-8-1919
Ham Lot 46 1876–1942
Metje Lot 46 1872–1943

TOLL, Christian Lot 3 11-6-1885 81 yrs.

TUITJER, Ted Lot 48 Baby

WALTERS, Fred Lot 22 1838–1915
Fred W. Lot 57 1875–1955
George (Baby son of F & C) Lot 23 1873 4 mo.
Kate Lot 22 1846–1918
Nora Lot 57 1887–1916

WILSON, Charles Lot 13 7-1-1871–2-10-1954
Dora Lot 13 (Wife of J.M.) 7-15-1838–7-21-1901
Esther Dora Lot 49 12-4-1892–12-13-1892
J.M. Lot 13 6-25-1828–12-16-1908
Mary Lot 1 (Wife of Frank E.) 9-11-1885–2-11-1909
Ray E. Lot 49 1890–1-3-1919 Age 23

WILTFANGS, Andrew Lot 16 (Son of Henry) 1915–1921

WURDINGER, Pauline Lot 62 1863–1932
Peter Lot 62 1872–1949

YARCHO, Emil W. Lot 11 1919
Grace May Lot 11 (Daug. of L & MC) 2-2-1886 2 mo. 15 days
Henrich Lot 11 (Son of H & S)
1863–10-7-1880 17 yr 10 mo
Henry Lot 11 4-17-1832–5-8-1927
Louis Lot 27 5-26-1861–1945
Lydia Louise (wife) Lot 10 (daug. of Emma & Herman Ruege) 5-16-1891–3-26-1974
Mary C. Lot 27 2-27-1862–1935
Sophia (wife) Lot 11 4-27-1837–5-8-1927
William Emil Lot 10 (Son of Sophia & Henry) 12-18-1874–5-15-1941
William & Lydia parents of Ruth, Floyd, Emil, Robert, Albert, Paul, Louise, Norma Lee

Additions

IMMING, Cora M. Lot 58 8-16-1883–4-3-1919
Engbert Lot 59 10-20-1848–1-6-1918
Henry Lot 58 1885–1980
Jess J. Lot 58 6-6-1889–4-3-1918
Sophia Lot 59 4-30-1857

KOHS, Anna Lot 41 10-15-1862–6-18-1897

KUSTER, Elisabeth Lot 7 D 1890 79 yrs.

POPE, Henry Lot 12 D 12-2-1895 68 yrs.
Elizabeth D 4-21-1891

Notes

Lot 29 is designated as pastor's
Lot 35 is designated as pauper lot
Lots 17, 18, 31, 52 and 60 through 70 are empty

HITESVILLE CEMETERY

There are very few records of the Hitesville Cemetery with dates. Among the early settlers in Ripley Township in 1855 were John and Christian Hites. John is buried in Section 20 and Christian in Section 28. In October 1855, the first burial took place. It was the small daughter of Samuel Kimmel. This was also the first death recorded for Ripley Township. The burial was made on what is known as the "Big Lot" south and east of the tree. On this lot are buried the families of Christian Hites, C.H. Kimmel, G.M. Graft, John Hites, Cid and Christian Stoners, Andrew and George Hesse and Patterson. When the original cemetery was platted is not known, but it was probably in the 1870s, as the first recordings of lots bear the dates of 1885. The east section was added in the early 1900s.

There are eleven servicemen buried in Hitesville. From the War of 1812 was Jacob Yost. From the Civil War were Jerry Margretz, George Wintz, Henry Gibson and Joe Considine. From World War I were Ed Langston, Emmet Graves, William Santee, Arthur Yost and Melvin Johnson. From World War II was Elmer Schriever.

Hitesville Cemetery is a township cemetery for the use of the surrounding territory. It is tax supported and under the direction of three trustees. It has never belonged to any church.

A new fence was erected in 1926 and replaced in 1964. In 1976, many of the older stones were repaired and reset. This project was financed by solicitations and donations.

Alberts, John F. 1858–1936 L173
Alberts, Vrouwtje 1856–1927 L173
Alberts, Albert son of F. & H. Alberts 1905–1927 L173
Alberts, Hauke 1879–1955 L173
Alberts, Folkert 1875–1958 L173
Alberts, Todd Kenneth son of Kenneth and Linda Dec 22, 1964–Sept 21, 1965 L174
Alberts, Harm 1917–1975 L182
Alberts, Bessie 1914–   L182
Alberts, Beverly Ann daug of Harm and Bessie 1940–1951 L182
Asche, Carl 1892–1974 L50
Asche, Dena 1895–1974 L50

Bakker, Tena 1892–1973 L46
Bakker, Henry 1882–1971 L48
Beaumont, Edmond E. 1869?–1973 L80
Beenken, Henry L. 1942–1953 L130
Beenken, Mary R. Feb 29, 1904 L130
Beenken, Lutjen, G. Jan 15, 1901–Nov 26, 1972 L130
Behrens, Richard 1895–1953 L129
Behrens, Tena 1900–1964 L129
Bohn, Charley 1887–1983 L94
Bohn, Grace 1889–1974 L94

Brinkman, Harm 1874–1961 L94

Brinkman, Anna A. 1883–1965 L25?

Brinkman, Jennie 1900–1983 L181

Brinkman, Chris 1899–   L181

Brinkman, Jacobus son of K. & K. b 1899 d Jan 30, 1900 L120

Brown, Bertha E. 1884–1960 L164

Brown, Norma L. 1935–1936 L184

Brown, Duwane T. 1913–1924 L184

Brown, Manlie 1873–1960 L70

Brown, Mother 1842–1932 L70 Large stone reads "Brown" Harrison born in Summerset Co Maine May 25, 1836 died Hitesville Butler Co Iowa. Jan. 3, 1901 L70

Brown, Father 1835–1901 L70

Christopherson, Daylen R. Oct 16, 1962–Sept 26, 1975 L175

Christopherson, Lawrence 1896–1970 L35

Christopherson, Leona 1899–   L35

Christopherson, Marlys Mae June 23, 1934 daug of Mr. and Mrs. L. Christopherson L35

Considine, Joseph Feb 20, 1845–July 9, 1908 Co K 147th Ill Vol Inf L171

Considine, Cathrine his wife Mar 30, 1855 Apr 1, 1908 L171

Considine, Andrew D. 1883–1958 L31

Considine, Pearl E. 1885–1957 L-31

Considine, Wayne R. 1915–1946 L31

Considine, Infant son of A. & P. 1909 L31

Considine, Infant daug of A. & P. 1907 L31

Considine, Infant daug of A. & P. 1910 L31

Considine, Marven 1888–1976 L183

Considine, Francis 1879–1941 L183

Considine, John 1826–1914 L172

Craft, Sue Ann 1933–1961 L7

Cripps, A.D. 1854–1885 L72

Crowson, Lillie M. 1900–   L188

Crowson, Harold I. 1897–   L188

Darlrymple, Alice E. d Apr 18, 1886 33Y 4m 11d L101

Davis, Lela Kay infant daug of George and Clara b Aug 5, 1906–d Aug 6, 1906 L107

Davis, Lucy J. wife of Jas. Mar 24, 1848–Mar 12, 1906 L63

Debur, Peter 1871–1940 L75

Debur, Lena 1881–1969 L75

Dennis, Father 1844–1922 L46

Dennis, Mother 1848–1890 L46 Tall stone in center reads Susie C. wife of R.A. d May 24, 1890 42y 5M 24d

Dennis, Henry E. d Oct 16, 1889 6y 6m 4d

Dennis, Susie F. d Jan 21, 1892 1y 8m 5d L46

Dennis, Henry E. 1883–1889 L46
Dennis, Susie F. 1890–1890 L46
Devries, George M. 1901–1938 L95
Devries, Sena 1921–   L188
Devries, Martin A. 1918–   parents of Gary and Ruth L188

Ellwood, Fred 1882–1943 L152
Ellwood, Jessie 1884–1929 L152
Eltjes, Florence H. 1900–   L1
Eltjes, Walter 1898–1951 L1
Eltjes, John 1867–1947 L33
Eltjes, Sepkea 1865–1941 L33
Epple, Ross 1935–1977 L186
Epple, Grace F. Feb 28, 1898–   L186
Epple, Theodore R. Feb 15, 1896 May 19, 1964 L186

Faint, Joseph 1894-1954 L155
Faint, Lou Amy 1894-1968 L155
Feckers, Malena 1892-1941 L79
Feckers, George 1885 -1952 L79
Feldman, Jessie daug of B.W. & M. d Aug 14, 1881 ly 8m 12d L30
Frey, George L. 1898-   L158
Frey, Johanna nee Meyer 1898–   L158

Gallagher, Laura M. 1899–1919 L9
Gibson, Clara 1880–1961 L133
Gibson, Harry G. 1883–1960 L133
Gibson, Francis W. son of H.G. & C. Apr 10, 1918–Jan 11, 1919 L133
Gibson, Dessie 1873–1918 L29
Gibson, Edgar W. 1871–1934 L29
Gibson, Son Keith 1912–1916 L29
Gibson, Infant son Vern L29
Gibson, Infant son Fern L29
Gibson, William H. large stone reads Co G 1 Mich Vol Lt Army William H. Gibson
    b Apr 26, 1833 d May 26, 1907
Gibson, Mary wife of William b Apr 27, 1851–d Nov 30, 1907 L35
Gibson, Father (G.A.R.) L135
Gibson, Mother L135
Gibson, Graves, Emmet Edward Iowa Pfc Co B 319 M.G.WWI b Mar 29, 1896–d
    Oct 20, 1968 L141
Gibson, Ethel G. b Dec 25, 1890–   L141
Green, Joseph b May 15, 1847 d Jan 1, 1898 L10
Green, Isaac W. b Jan 3, 1843 d Sept 29, 1886 L1O
Green, Unmarked foot stone L10
Green, Mary A. b 1853 d 1930 L10

Green, Mary b Aug 5, 1812 d Oct 25, 1899 L10
Green, Mother Maggie 1869–1955 L27
Green, Large stone reads "Green"
Green, Orin J. 1859–1911 L27
Green, James H. son of O.J. & M.M. d Dec 7, 1898 8m 8d L27
Green, Jimmie d Sept 1, 1886 2y 6m L28
Green, Eliott Lee d Sept 29, 1886 3m 15d L28
Groen, Herman 1887–1976 L94
Groen, Maggie 1889–1967 parents of Grace, Alice and William L94
Groothuis, Alrich 1880–1966 L108
Groothuis, Minnie 1881–1966 L108
Groothuis, Fred A. 1908–   L176
Groothuis, Frieda 1910–   parents of Orville, Larrie and Lorna L176
Groothuis, Herman A. 1912–1959 L176
Groothuis, Helen W. 1916–   Married Mar 12, 1937 L165

Haan, Fred 1912–   L60
Haan, Mabel 1910–   L60
Haan, Maggie 1887–1975 L48
Haan, John H. 1882–1971 L48
Halterman, Mother Susan E. Langston 1893–1958 L30
Hane, Anna wife of D. Hane d Sept 22, 1884 56y 6m 6d L30
Hane, Luthere daug of D. & A. Hane d May 11, 1884 17y L4
Harm, Martha Jane 1946–1947 L156
Harms, Harm 1897–   L4
Harms, Margaret 1899–1948 L4
Herr, Mable Hites 1882–1952 L78
Hesse, Andrew b Sept 14, 1819 d June 30, 1897 L74 C-S
Hesse, Catharine b May 25, 1832–d Oct 3, 1899 L74C-S There is one large stone
    and individual headstone, this is about a 24 ft. lot with a cement frame around it.
Hesse, Chester A.J. son of A. & C. d May 2, 1863 L74C-S
Hesse, Lewis b Nov 4, 1852 d Oct 18, 1882 L74C-S
Hesse, George H. 1876–1933 L151
Hesse, Vina R. 1873–1966 L151
Hicks, Martha 1809–1874 L105
Hicks, Rezin 1834-1892 L105
Hites, Albert E. 1864–1949 L99
Hites, Mary L. 1873–1954 L99
Hites, Ivan son of A.E. & M.L. Nov 21, 1900 L99
Hites, one flat stone with "G.H." L38
Hites, Mother Grace Hites 1902–1969 L25
Hites, Mary Ann wife of J.C. Hites d Aug 16, 1880 49y 6m 13d L73
Hites, William H. son of J.C. & M.A. d Oct 6, 1881 12y 8m 14d L73
Hites, Nancy wife of J.C. Hites d Apr 2, 1895 64y L73
Hites, John C. d Aug 22, 1899 76y 1m 18d L74A-N

Hites, Nancy E. Sept 2, 1867 9d L74A-N

Hites, George W. d Nov 30, 1866 8m 12d L74A-N (George and Nancy E. children of J. & C. Hites)

Hites, Catharine wife of Jonathan d Oct 18, 1888 63Y 1m 6d L74A-N Small stone "Mother" E74A-N

Hites, Nancy E. (unreadable) L74A-N

Hites, George W. L74A-N

Hites, Christin d June 28, 1861 L74A-N

Hites, Levi b May 11, 1832 d Jan 30, 1909 L154

Hites, Christina wife of Levi b July 28, 1827 d Mar 11, 1914 L154

Hites, Richard A. b 1864 d 1937 L154

Hites, Gladys 1908–19 L187

Hites, Clifford 1902–1977 L187

Hites, Cora N. daug of J.W. & M. d Aug 20, 1884 1?y 1m L101

Hites, W.W. son of J.W. & M. d Mar 29, 1884 33Y 3m 11d L101

Hites, Lewis D. 1907–1962 L98

Hites, Minnie 1919–   parents of Lois, Roger and Ricky L98

Hites, Eva May 1893–1963 L98

Hites, Maud 1888-1973 L169

Hites, Percy L. 1884–1939 L169

Hites, George D. 1856–1920 L168

Hites, Wm. E. 1860–1944 L77

Hites, Lucy wife of W.E. 1869–1924 L77 Large stone reads "Hites" no other L77

Hites, Lura daug of W.S. & L.L. 1899–1900 L77 Large stone reads "Hites" L78

Hites, Rosa M. daug of L.C. & D.V. Nov 21, 1884

Hites, John W. Dec 12, 1825–Mar 22, 1906 L102

Hites, Mary wife of John W. Feb 2, 1832–July 24, 1912 L102

Hites, Wallace A. 1871–1955 L102

Hites, Nanie N. 1876–1963 L155

Hites, Jasper B. 1862–1952 L155

Hites, Louisa J. 1873–1951 L155

Hites, John unmarked stone—funeral marker 1911–1911 L156

Hites, Minnie 1891–1980 L156

Hites, Tjeodore 1880–1948 L49

House, Marjorie 1958–1961 L49

Jacobs, Frank C. 1892–1975 L99

Jacobs, Alberta 1902–1976 L99

Jay, Isabelle daug of H.B. & E. Jay d Mar 11, 1872 1d L74B-S

Johnson, Kuno D. 1912–1965 L158

Johnson, Kathryn 1904–   L158

Johnson, Melvin 1897–1969 Funeral Marker, WWI Marker and WWII Marker L140

Johnston, William E. son of James P. & E.S. d Sept 19, 1899 2m 18d L106

Johnston, M.L.K. on stone with no dates L106

Johnston, Unmarked stone L106

Junker, Tena Schneiderman wife of Henry Junker 3-29-1884 to 2-3-1943 (Mother of Tony, John, Reints, Henry, Olive, William, Herman, August and Bennie) L47
Junker, Henry husband of Tena (stone also lists children) 7-27-1877–3-12-1948 L47
Junker, Reints 1909–1975 L47

Kampman, Kate Eltjes Sept 26, 1889 May 10, 1949 L33
Kappel, Hermann 1914– L184
Kappel, George J. 1898–1968? L185?
Kappel, J.B. b Nov 8, 1904 d Apr 20, 1923 L184
Kappel, Bertha 1874–1953 L185
Kappel, John G. 1864–1923 L185
Kimmel, Margaret L. d Sept 7, 1855 l?y 4d L74A-S
Kimmel, James B. d Mar 28, 1861 1m 11d children of S. & J. Kimmel L74A-S
Kimmel, Jane wife of Samuel d Sept 10, 1868 54y 7m 26d L74A-S
Kimmel, Samuel 1813–1881 L74A-S
Kimmel, Betsy d Jan 16, 1900 79y 9m 15d L74A-S
Kimmel, Sammie son of J.W. & E.M. Kimmel Feb 16, 1872–Aug 17, 1875 L103
Kimmel, Initials only M.L K. no dates L106
Kincaid, Edwin d Sept 12, 1886 61y 5m 17d L43
Kincaid, Catherine wife of Edwin d Aug 29, 1886 L43
Kincaid, Edwin son of E. & C. d Aug 1879?
Kincaid, Little Jennie daug of E.M. & A.C. d Sept 4, 1886 10m 6d L65
Kincaid, Elizabeth F. wife of Louis J. d Apr 21, 1885 32y 3m 4d L66
Kincaid, Flat stone unreadable L66
Kincaid, Ray son of L.J. & E. d Feb 7, 1879
Kluiter, Jerry 1882–1961 L3
Kluiter, Tetje 1884–1948 L3
Krushwitz, Henry H. 1835–1901 funeral home marker L97

Langston, Edwin A. Father 1888–1943 Private Div 1 64th Spruce Sqd'n N WWI L30
Langston, M. Duane son 1921–1937 L30
Langston, Infant son 1916 L30
Lincoln, Elen B. daug of O.H. & E.A. Lincoln d May 24, 1884 1m 21d L76
Lindaman, Marie 1883–1954 L61
Lindaman, Dick 1873–1956 L61
Linn, Sarah S. July 3, 1875 Jan 12, 1909 L138
Linn, Joseph S. June 23, 1874 Dec 7, 1910 L138
Linn, Joseph July 28, 1834 Nov 23, 1907 L153
Linn, Large "Linn" stone L153
Linn, Rachel E. Aug 18, 1845 Mar 22, 1910 L153
Lewis, Francis V. 1914–1931 L11
Lewis, Orton & Orlo Apr 1, 1915 L11
Lewis, Arthur E. Oct 11, 1911–Jan 9, 1912 L11
Lewis, Francis M. 1930–1932 L26
Lewis, Everette G. 1934–1935 L26

Lewis, George A. 1878–1962 L26
Lewis, Ida M. 1883–1973 L26
Lewis, Mother Tillie F. 1879–   L24
Lewis, Glen E. 1901–1963 L24
Lowery, James E. 1866–1927 L37
Lowery, Baby Lowery 1899 L37
Lubben, Mother Maggie 1887–1967 L96
Lubben, Son John 1909–1967 L96
Lubben, Father Albert 1882–1976 L96

Maifield, William L. 1894–1974 L39
Maifield, Alda V. 1898–1978 L39
Margretz, Cecil A. 1914–1954 L32 Funeral home marker Margretz 1881–1951 L32
Margretz, Duane R. 1905–1907 L32
Margretz, Anna 1880–1935 L32
Margretz, Guy C. 1872–1938 L41
Margretz, J.S. Sept 29, 1838 June 3, 1901 L41
Margretz, Mary Elizabeth wife of J.S. Sept 11, 1830–Mar 11 1901 L41
Margretz, Herman E. son of J.S. & M.E. Sept 16, 1870 June 20, 1890 L41
Martin, Isabella E. wife of J.L. b Apr 2, 1868 d Feb 14, 1895 L63
Martin, Infant daug of J.L. & I.E. b Dec 30, 1889 d Apr 17, 1890 L63
Matty, Charles V. 1899–1983 L170
Matty, Anna V. 1897–1956 L170
McF., A. no dates L137
McFarland, Mary wife of Andrew b Jan 29, 1821 d Jan 3, 1886 L136
McFarland, Andrew b Mar 25, 1823 d Nov 13, 1902 L136
McGruder, Mildred Hites 1911–   L76
McLaren, Harold 1930–1931 L34
McLaren, Freda 1905–   L34
McLaren, Geo. Vernon 1900–1975 L34
McLaren, John 1865–1944 L68
McLaren, Rachel 1876–1967 L68
Mehmen, Infant son of J. & A. 1923 L185
Mennenga, Mary E. 1912–1964 L62
Mennenga, George 1905–1983 L62
Moore, Elmer L. 1902–1934 L139
Moore, Freda A. 1899–1918 L139
Moore, Lizzie Hites 1862–1943 L169
Moye, Baby Boy 1966 L60
Mulder, Hendrik 1895–1966 L189
Mulder, Larry W. son of William and Minnie July 29–Sept 3, 1942 L189
Mulder, Minnie 1904–   L189
Mulder, William 1898–1982 parents of Berniece, Arthur, Ilene, Larry and DeAnne
    L189

Naber, Dena H. 1899–1933 L6
Naber, Treantje Kate 1877–1960 L157
Naber, Gerit G. 1875–1952 L157
Neuberger, Anna Einger wife of L. d Aug 13, 1899 16y 4m 11d L64

Orvis, Albert B. son of W.B. & L.O. d Oct 9, 1886 1y 1m 1d L103
Orvis, Mother Nell 1849–1941 L103
Orvis, George son 1868–1942 L103
Oxford, Anna May daug of W.H. & A.A. d Sept 17, 1880 2y 9d L77

Patterson, Kaziah E. daug of D.C. & L.E. d July 22, 1871 1y 4m 11d L74D-N
Patten, Gertrude E. 1873–1937 L150
Patten, Edward A. 1862–1937 L150
Pike, Randy J. Sept 25, 1958 Mar 14, 1959 L12

Reed, Garfield 1882–1962 L128
Reed, Anna 1886 L128
Rottink, Elizabeth G. 1892–   L159
Rottink, Henry D. 1888–1982 L159

Safford, Rosetta Lowery 1870–1923 L37
Santee, Velma M. 1910–   L8
Santee, Herbert G. 1906–   L8
Santee, Lee 1898 L9
Santee, Charles 1901–1902 L9
Santee, George 1861–1932 L9
Santee, Matilda 1874–1949 L9
Santee, Joseph W. F 1 US Navy Jan 17, 1894–June 13, 1974 L201
Schriever, Fred H. 1882–1951 L140
Schriever, Dora 1903–1975 L140
Schriever, Elmer H. Iowa Private Co I 38 Inf Div Korea PH Apr 2, 1928–Sept 10, 1950 L140
Shafer, Florance May Jan 8, 1891 Aug 6, 1891 L101
Shafer, Leroy Aug 28, 1893 Sept 22, 1896 children of N. & E. Shafer L101
Shafer, F.M.S. no dates L100
Shafer, L.S. no dates L100
Shaffer, Willis son of Thos J. & Annie B. Feb 20, 1905–Apr 11, 1905 L134

Shaffer, Mary daug of Thos. J. & Annie B. May 11, 1908–Mar 23, 1908 L134
Shaffer, Large stone that reads "Shaffer"
Shaffer, Thos J. Mar 14, 1872 June 7, 1959 L134
Sluiter, Anna 1876–1964 L36
Sluiter, Jacob 1877–1968 L36
Smith, Theresa Mae 1885–1962 L24
Smith, Henry E. 1878–1982 L24

Smith, Wilhelmina 1885–1967 L50
Smith, George E. 1881–1969 L50
Spieker, Anna 1907–   L190
Spieker, Jerry F. 1905–1982 L190
Straite, Rose F. daug of Mr. & Mrs. W.R. d Feb 27, 1887 1m 25d L111
Street, Bert O. June 7, 1889 Feb 11, 1964 L81
Street, Addie L. July 2, 1888 Feb 1963 L81
Stoner, Asa 1845–1916 L69
Stoner, Mary 1848–1915 L69
Stoner, Mother no dates L69
Stoner, Father no dates L69
Stoner, Geo. W. Sept 29, 1872 57y 11m 15d L74B-N
Stoner, Delila wife of Geo. W. d Dec 8, 1874 45y 3m 2d L74B-N
Stoner, Eli David 1863–1869 L74B-N
Stoner, Christian d Dec 26, 1890 43y 11m 11d L74B-N (L74B-N is framed with
    cement and is about 24 ft. in size)
Stoner, Merta Nov 19, 1890–Mar 20, 1891 L71
Stoner, Jessie A. May 1–1890 Mar 20, 1891 L71
Stoner, Val Feb 16, 1884–Oct 6, 1885 L71 Children of Ira and Bertha Stoner

Tack, Margaret 1909–   L190
Tack, Harvey 1908–   L190
Taft, Joan 1854–1881 (believe the old stone reads Taft, Joanne daug of J.W. & M.
    Hites d Oct 5, 1881 27y 5m 15d)
Trimble, David 1861–1924 L72 Large stone reads "Trimble" L72
Trimble, Josephine Crips 1860–1950 L72

Uhlenhopp, Jake R. 1903–1960 L81
Uhlenhopp, Chas. R. 1910–   L81
Uhlenhopp, Grace 1903–1984 L5
Uhlenhopp, Chris 1898–1982
Uhlenhopp, Johanna 1876–1959 L5
Uhlenhopp, Robert 1874–1946 L5
Uhlenhopp, LaVon 1934–   L6
Uhlenhopp, Ed R. 1916–   L6
Uhlenhopp, C. Elizabeth 1918–1981 L13
Uhlenhopp, Robert 1907–1971 L13
Uhlenhopp, Johanna daughter 1938–1964 L13
Uhlenhopp, Martha Feb 23, 1890 Feb 10, 1976 L62
Uhlenhopp, Ed Sept 17, 1885 July 4, 1954 L62
Uhlenhopp, Rena 1908–   L149
Uhlenhopp, Chris H. Nov 29, 1902 Oct 1, 1970 L164
Uhlenhopp, Sander 1895–1970 L164
Uhlenhopp, Sena 1912–   L164
Uhlenhopp, Nellie d Feb 4, 1984

Wagner, Margaret 1875–1962 L172 Baby Wagner 1912 L172
Wagner, Chasper 1871–1960 L172
Wheeler, Jesse Edwin son of ??? L104
Wheeler, Josephene 1886–1916 L40
Wheeler, Wilkenson, Mable B. 1883–1964 L108
Wheeler, David E. 1876–1947 L108
Wildeboer, Henry 1865–1941 L112
Williams, Mother Mable Yost 1892–1934 L167
Wintz, Margaret A. 1876–1974 L170
Wintz, Elmer E. 1868–1956 L170
Wintz, Henrietta Mar 20, 1842 Mar, 1912 L63
Wintz, Geo. W. Oct 22, 1838 d May 1906 Co B 116th Ohio L63

Yost, Arthur Elmer Private 50 Co 20 Regt Engrs WWI Aug 25, 1896–May 14, 1971 L166
Yost, Chauncey 1899–1974 L166
Yost, Anna M. 1899–19 L166
Yost, Guy 1886–1972 L166
Yost, Vera 1891–1938 L166
Yost, Elmer E. 1863–1946 L167
Yost, Carrie C. 1864–1949 L167
Yost, Gladys E. daug of Elmer and Carrie Yost b May 29, 1907 d Nov 24, 1907 5m 20d L167
Yost, Hattie A. 1893–19 L157
Yost, Ray 1891–1973 L157
Yost, Infant daug of Edwin and Mabel d May 5, 1903 L67
Yost, Aurilla C. June 4, 1851 July 28, 1942 L67
Yost, Large stone reads "Yost"
Yost, Charles K. Mar 28, 1845 Dec 6, 1929 L67
Yost, Ethel daug of C.K. & A.C. Yost d Mar 27, 1882 1y 10m 13d L67
Yost, Cora May daug of C.K. & A.C. Yost d Dec 4, 1877 4y 10m 2d L67
Yost, Jacob b Oct 9, 1809 d June 24, 1891 81y 8m 15d Veteran of War of 1812 L68
Yost, Evaline E. wife of Jacob Yost d Oct 16, 1888 48y 16d L68
Yost, Edwin K. Dec 15, 1876–Jan 22, 1964 L42
Yost, Mable A. Oct 3, 1879 Nov 13, 1980 L42 parents of Ivan, Kenneth, Edyth, Ralph, Florence, John and Alice

Others Believed to Be Buried in the Hitesville Cemetery but Without Stones

Johnston, Iona Isabel obituary reads age 2 last March, youngest child of Mr. and Mrs. J.P. Johnston. Probably buried in L106

Moon, James born Jan 8, 1885 at Dumont. Died June 4, 1910. Probably buried in L171 which is owned by his uncle.

Fern, Edith nee Shaffer born Nov 14, 1910. Died May 7, 1969. Ashes buried in Hitesville Cemetery, probably in L134

Hites, Catherine wife of Joseph Rites Born about 1842. Died about 1915. Probably buried in L100
Hites, Joseph born 1834-35 died Nov 11, 1935 age 96y 8m 22d probably in L100

(Information received from Velma Lettington, daughter of Kesley Hites, lists that the following are buried in L38.)
Hites, Kesley Grant 1867–1948
Hites, Martha Jane Champion 1872–1962 wife of Kesley
Hites, William Levi b & d Sept 27, 1903
Hites, Infant Girl
Hites, Almeda b about 1908
Hites, Wayne b about 1911

(Information received from Ruth Hickman, daughter of Kesley Hites, lists that the following are buried in L38.)
Hites, Kesley Grant Father
Hites, Martha Jane Champion Mother
Hites, Levi Grant born Hitesville
Hites, Zelma born Hitesville
Hites, Naomi born Pleasantville, Iowa
Hites, Wayne born near Waverly, Virginia about 1909

Taylor, Janie youngest of the nine children of Mr. and Mrs. E. Taylor d Dec 10, 1883. Obituary reads buried in Hitesville.

MADISON TOWNSHIP CEMETERY, SITE OF VILLAGE OF CLUTTERVILLE

This cemetery was platted in 1873 by M.D.L. Niece under the auspices of the Madison Cemetery Association. This association was composed of the leading citizens of the town, among whom were: W. Watson, J. Baker, S. Harvey, T.W. Smith, J. Brooks, M. Harvey, J.O. Slade, J. Kalabarer, A. Schmitz, Frank Beach, P. Long and P. Pfaltgraftz. The first burial was the remains of Mrs. Jacob Kalabarer.

KIRBY, Mary Agnes, daug. of John J. & Ellen A. Kirby died Aug. 18, 1886 age 6 mo.
RITZMAN, Jackson died Aug. 5, 1886 age 13ys 11mo 15 ds
SLAID, Emily J. wife of O.F. Slaid died Oct 8, 1886 aged 66y 9m 2d

Large Watson stone with FATHER headstone on north side and MOTHER headstone on south side of the large stone. Large stone reads:

W. WATSON July 11, 1821 Dec. 3, 1912

ALBATINA wife of W. Watson Mar. 22, 1829–July 1, 1901

South of the MOTHER headstone:

Dr. L.O. WATSON 1861–1926

South of above stone:

GILBERT N. son of W. & A. Watson 1845–1896

Co. D 46th WI. Vol. Infantry

SMITH, Samuel J. died Mar. 8, 1872 age 44y 1m 6d

MACK, William H. 1823–1896 age 72y 8m 18d

MACK, A. wife of W.H. Mack 1823–

REINERS, Teddina ehefrau von R. Reiners Gest. 14 Marz 1903 Aller 28 Jahre, 11 monate In Meines vater's haus, sind viele, wohnungen

REINERS, Siena Mar. 12, 1910 Apr. 19, 1912

REINERS, Sophia Mar. 12, 1911 May 12, 1912

BRUSE, Martje Geb Brinkman Geb 27 Marz 1851 Gest 5 Feb 1890

EYGABROAD, Luella J. daug. of G.H. & A.E. Eygabroad died Feb 16, 1891 aged 17y 5m 1d

HARTGRAVES, Estella daug. of N. & S. Hargraves died Nov. 24, 1887 age 16y 9m 10d

HARTGRAVES, Nicholas (same stone) died Apr. 1, 1888 aged 69y 7m 14d

ETZEN, Wilhelm Sept. 9, 1881 June 11, 1925

The following names were listed in the 1940 WPA records of Butler Co. cemeteries. No stones found.

BARTH, Christina 1889–1913

CLARKE, Charles J. 1858–1914

LOWELL (LOWTOWN) CEMETERY

Southeast of Clarksville in Butler Township is a cemetery that dates back to 1852, known as Lowell Cemetery. In the early 1850s, a hunter and trapper by the name of Carpenter and his family built a cabin and dug a well but did not bother to register their land with the government. During this time, two members of his family died and were buried in a southeast corner of the present site of the Lowell Cemetery.

Herman Hunt came to Butler County from Ohio in the spring of 1853. He had with him a Military Land Warrant for eighty acres of land in Section 28 of Butler Township. He located the land and then traveled to Dubuque to have the land registered in his name, as there were no county seats established in nearby counties at that time.

Lowell Town Cemetery. *Taken by Jim Gates, 2008, used with his permission.*

In 1855, Herman Hunt sold the land to John Hickle of Normal, Illinois. He set aside an acre of ground as a community cemetery, as the Carpenter family had requested the site of the two graves always be protected. Later, an additional half acre was added to the original plot.

In recent years, unmarked graves have been marked and records brought up to date. This has taken a lot of research, and the officers are commended for their efforts to record the happenings of the early day settlers of Butler Township. These can be found in the *Cemetery Record of Butler County* vol. 1, published by the Butler County Historical Society in 1987. A new addition to the cemetery was just recently added, and new burials occur there every year.

Veterans Buried in the Lowell Cemetery

<u>Mexican War</u>
David Van Gundy

<u>Civil War</u>
Charles Mix
Byron Reynolds
Wm. Flood
Hiram Poisol
Andrew McElhaney
Orville Calkins
Edwin Wilkinson
J.H. Hickle
Alfred Hickle
J.D. Roberts

World War I
Fred Ling
Bennie Oster
Sam Drenth
Cecil Sturdevant
Howard Culver
Ward Harris

World War II
James Roberts (buried in Germany)
Ike Hilton
James Wilcox
Charles Drenth
Elmer Pat Wilcox
Ray Tamm
Harry Peterson

Burials are current only to 1998.

ABBEY, Mr. and Mrs. No first names or dates C-20
ABBOTT, Gracie B. June 30, 1894 Feb 10, 1895 C-19
ADAIR, Forest C. 1907—parents of Roma and Terry S-20
Marian A. 1913—S-20
ALLEN, George no dates S-8
ANDERSON, Steven R. son of R.L. & S.J. d Nov 8, 1951 S-12
ARMSTRONG, four graves. No first names or dates S-22
John, Mar 17, 1800 Apr 17, 1873 73 years, 1 month S-23
Mrs. John, no first name or dates S-23

BALL, Clarence F-1905—C-6
Doris R. 1907—C-6
Grace Loomis Ball 1902–1971 C-22
BALLOU, Infant no dates S-24
BARKELEW, Guy son of S. & M.E. d Jan 26, 1879 3 wks ld C-5
Infant, no dates C-5
BETTS, Charles son of C. & L.E. d Feb 10, 1866 8m 5d C-4
Christopher, Father d Feb 17, 1899 69 years "In my Father's house are many mansions." "In labor and in love allied, In death they here sleep, side by side. Resting in peace the aged twain. Till Christ shall raise them up again." C-4
Infant of C. & L.E. d May 1, 1870. "Our little children have gone to rest. God called them home; He thought it best." C-4

Lucinda E. wife of Christopher, Mother d Jan 3, 1894 58y "Precious one from us has gone. A voice we loved is stilled. A place is vacant in our home which never can be filled." C-4

Sarah E. 1859–1938 C-4

William H. 1859–1939 C-4

BILLHIMER, Barbara, wife of John, d Dec 8, 1861? 66y lm 11d (stone old & broken) S-5

BLANCHARD, Bunny Lynn May 3, 1977 July 4, 1977 S-3

BLEIER, Mae 1874–1947 S-14

BOHLEN Family stone N-14

Harriet 1930—N-14

Jeffrey Allen Infant 1959 N-14

Oren 1930–1967 N-14

BOLIN, Clement M. 1912–1975 father of Joselyn, Rosalee, Patricia, and Priscilla N-5

Elmer N. 1890–1966 S-7

Family stone N-4

Floyd Jr. Apr 13, 1967 N-3

Glenn (infant) 1931 N-4

Harold 1932-1938 N-4

Infant "C." N-5

Lucy M. 1891–1971 S-7

Robert E. July 15, 1939 d Mar 28, 1968 N-4

BOUKAS, Nellie Marquand born in Clarksville, IA 1890, married William Bourkas in Marion, IA 1921 Died here 1939 C-14

BOWEN Family stone   S-15

John Mar 30, 1826 Nov 10, 1905 S-15

Mary A. Mar 5, 1830 May 17, 1902 S-15

BOYD, Hugh A. 1861–1929 C-3

John father 1834–1922 C-2

Mariah mother 1837–1918 C-2

Rachel L. mother 1867–1948 C-3

BRAGG, Mrs. Olive d Dec 5, 1881 32 yr 1 m 24d C-15

BRANDOS, Ethel A. 1903—C-5

Floyd D. 1906–1966 C-5

Infant (no dates) C-5

BROCKELMAN, John 1890–1936 C-19

BROWN, "Children" no dates C-5

BURK, Earl infant son of C. & N.E. d Apr 17, 1889 7m 3d C-16

BURKE, "Child" no dates C-16

Eliza 1887 C-16

James E. 1831–1911 S-2

James H. son of J.E. & M.J., d June 21, 1863 6y lm S-2

John H. 1853–1888 S-2

Mary J. his wife 1831–1917 S-2

William 1890 C-16

BUSS, Gretje Mother 1829–1913 C-11

CALKINS, Emma wife of Orville d Aug 19, 1899 43y 9m 30d. "A precious one from us has gone, A voice we loved is stilled. A place is vacant in our home, Which never can be filled." S-2

Lora E. d Feb 13, 1883 5m 13d S-2.

Orville W. 8 ILL Cav WWI S-2

CAMPBELL, Alvin 1887–1983 S-9

Opal 1891–1956

CARPENTER, "Children" 1851 first graves in Lowtown Cemetery. S-25

CATCHPOOL, E. Grace 1877–1966 S-12

Henry F. 1872–1946 married 1903 parents of Elizabeth, Maurice, Herbert, and Roger S-12

Maurice G. July 5, 1905 June 21, 1943 son of Henry and Grace S-12

Roger H. 1911—S-11

Viola C. 1906–1971 S-11

CHAMPLIN, Abbie F-1858–1915 C-20

Alpha A.E. 1866–1942 C-20

Family stone C-20

Lovina N. 1834–1905 C-20

John B. 1807–1881 C-

COLVER, DeWitt L. 1801–1869 S-7

Phineas E. 1872–1896 S-8

Sophronia 1806–1899 S-7

COOK, Alonzo H. Lon 1904–1970 C-19

Donald V. 1928—C-19

Family stone C-19

Gladys L. 1903–1986 C-19

Patricia L-1928—C-19

COPELAND, Ann L. 1945–1978 S-10

Arland died 1913 S-10

Emily Copeland Couch Mother 1850–1908 C-6

Family stone C-6

Freddie G. d Apr 25, 1878 1y 8m 13d "In that heavenly mansion above, He is waiting to welcome us home." C-6

G. Arnold 1913–1965 S-10

Infant (no dates) S-18

Ira A. 1879–1957 S-10

Leslie 1908—C-6

Loretta 1906—C-6

Lulu 1882–1972 S-10

Willis D. Father d Nov 16, 1888 36y 5m 16d C-6

CULVER, Fred 1874–1967 S-8

Howard E. PFC US ARMY WWI July 20, 1896 May 24, 1984 S-9

Lela Dec 6, 1895 Dec 12, 1895 S-8

CURRY, Elizabeth E.-daug of T. & M.A. d June 22, 1886 37y 8m 18d C-3

Family stone C-3

Mary A. Mother d Jan 31, 1884 73y 6m 3d C-3

Ruann daug of T. & M.A. d Apr 14, 1878 22y 15d "We mourn because she's left us, So early thus in life. But he who hath bereft us, Hath freed from sin and strife." C-3

Thomas Father d July 29, 1883 72y 4m 21d

DANIELS, Mr. and Mrs. No first names or dates C-19

DEARTH, Isaac 1826–1892 C-5

Nancy wife of Isaac d Sept 22, 1886 63y 7m 17d

"Oh our loved and only Mother, Never shall my soul forego, Those fond ties that death has severed. With the ruthless grasp of woe." C-5

DELKER, George W. 1864–1917 C-2

Ida M. 1874–1973 C-2

Family stone C-2

Ruth 1906–1948 C-2

DOUGLAS, no first name or dates S-11

DRENTH, Charley MO PRIVATE 35 B N 8 Sig Tng Regt WWII Sept 4, 1902–Nov 2, 1970 C-17

Elizabeth 1897–1950 C-17

Family stone C-17

Sam. IA PFC US ARMY WWI Sept 13, 1895–Oct 31, 1971 C-17

ERNST three graves. No first names or dates. S-21

FAIRBURN, Mr. and Mrs. No first names or dates S-5

FLEMING, Mayme M.1895–1948 S-8

FLOOD, Baby. No first name or dates. S-22

Delia V. Mother Feb 24, 1839–Oct 10, 1916 S-22

Family stone C-20 & S-22

George E. Mar 9, 1860 Apr 20, 1936 C-20

Lizzie M. Jan 28, 1867 Feb 18, 1903 S-22

Lucy Emillie wife of G.E. Sept 9, 1865 Apr 22, 1919 C-20

Nettie L. Nov 11, 1875–Aug 28, 1933 S-22

William Father d Feb 16. 1898, 68y CO E 32 IA Civil War S-22

FOKKENA, Wilhelm Heinrich 1953–1970 C-13

FORRY, Archie D. 1884–1958 C-15

Charlotte M. 1883–1958 C-16

Family stone—C-15 & C-16

Frank 11. 1873–1953 C-16

Jessie V. 1882–1968 C-15

Shane F. 1970 son of Kenneth and Jean C-16

FRANKLIN, Benjamin son of C. & N.D Sept 17, 1867 25y 5m 3d C-5

David d Apr 2, 1875 75y "My trust is in God" C-7

Sarah J. wife of T. Franklin July 19, 1830 Apr 21, 1904 C-5

Taylor 1848–1920 C-5

FRYE, Bert two graves no dates C-12

GATES, Caroline Mother Jan. 21, 1818 Mar 9, 1903 S-4.

Christianna W. daug of J. & C.D Feb 2, 1871 15y 3m 18d S-3

Elizabeth E. daug of J. & C.D Nov 13, 1870 21y 10m 17d S-3

Infant no dates S-3

Johnson, Father d Mar 26, 1872. 52y 5m 9d S-4

Mary E. daug of J. & C. d Sept 26, 1865 1m 20d S-3

GREGG, Two Children no dates C-6

Robert d Apr 13, 1881 79y C-6

GROEN, Annetta G. 1923—parents of Randell N-13

Dena Mother 1896–1934 S-14

Family stone N-13

Leona, J. 1918—S-14

Raymond L. 1920—N-13

Wilbur E. 1914—parents of James, Wilson, Barbara S-14

HARKEN, Henrietta 1888–1963 C-4

I.U. 1885–1960 C-4

Melvin E. 1919–1942 C-4

HARRIS Family stone N-12

Hilda A. 1901—N-12

Josie 1853–1903 S-6

M.G. 1851–1921 S-6

Susannah 1824–1903 S-6

Ward E. 1892–1985 parents of Ward Jr, Bud, Ladyne, Jim N-12

HICKLE, Alfred Father PRIVATE CO G 8 REGT IA CAV Civil War March 2, 1846, Jan 18, 1933 S-1

Alma G. 1874–1961 C-1

Anna Mother 1852–1937 S-1

Arthur son of S. & H.E. d Sept 4, 1875 1y 2m C-4

David V. Mar 9, 1848 June 16, 1907 C-1

Eliza Ann 1857–1939 C-1

Elizabeth Mc D. Mother 1848–1935 C-1

Emma J. Mar 26, 1858 Dec 1, 1927 C-1

Family stone C-1 and C-16 & C-7

Floyd 1884–1942 C-16

Frank son of W.H. & L.H. d May 29, 1870 3m 14d C-2

Grace L. Our Darling Youngest daug of J.H. & L. d Jan 24, 1892. 11y 6m 8d C-1

Henry d Feb 5, 1884 62y C-1

Hester Mother July 7, 1820–June 26, 1910 C-1

James D. d Nov 15, 1885 22y 3m 9d "One less to love on earth. One more to meet in Heaven." C-7

James Warren 1854–1940 C-1

Jessie daug of J.H. & E.D. May 22, 1879 2d C-1

J.H. Father 1841–1927 CO E 32 IA Infantry Civil War C-1

John Father Aug 24, 1812 Dec 16, 1894 C-1
Mary J. Mother d May 6, 1900 77y 11m 28d C-7
May daug of W.H. & L.M. d Mar 19, 1874 3y 1m 1d C-2
Norma 1892–1981 C-16
Reason Father d Nov 8, 1889 69y 6m 7d C-7
HILTON, Irvin R. IA TM1 US Navy WWII Jun 29, 1901 Sept 18, 1973 C-21
HOWDEN, Infant child of John
Howden (no dates) C-13
HUNT Family stone C-18
Herman S. 1878–1967 C-1
M. LaVerne 1878–1968 C-18
Neal 1920–1926 C-18
HUSBAND, Clara M. d May 2, 1867 18y 11m S-4
John B. brother d Nov 30, 1886 29y 9m S-4

JANSSEN Family Stone C-13
JANKEN mother 1834–1919 C-13
John father 1834–1915 C-13
Kasjen husband 1881–1948 C-13
Wilheimine wife 1887–1935 C-13
JASPERS, Ben R June 22, 1871–Mar. 20, 1960 C-11
Berend M. son of B.R. & G. geb 7 Dez 1911 gest 15 Okt 1918 C-11
Berend M-father June 22, 1836–June 3, 1910 C-12
Edde H. July 24, 1880 June 18, 1945 C-12
Grace J. May 11, 1881 Oct 29, 1961 parents of Berend M., Gertie, Minnie & Johanna C-11
Harm E. geb den 27 June 1883 gest den 2 June 1905. ruhe Sanft (rest, sleep softly) C-12
Jakomina H-mother May 19, 1842–Apr 29, 1929 Ruhe Sanft in Frieden (rest, sleep softly in peace) C-12
Minnie July 25, 1874 June 4, 1934 C-12

KNAPP, Infant (no dates) C-16
KNIGHT, Darrell E. son of W.J. 1902–1919 C-7
Henry Feb 7, 1828–Oct 16, 1909
Infant son of H. & S. Oct 15, 1870 d Oct 17, 1870 C-7
John son of Henry & Sarah d Jun 3, 1878 16y 4m 5d C-7
Sarah wife of Henry d Oct 24, 1892 62y 6m 25d
"Weep not dearest children, I have left you for a happier home. And in heaven I'll bid you welcome, For I'm only going home. All my trials and cares are over; I'm numbered with the blest I have reached my golden City Where there is eternal rest." C-7
W.J. 1867–1922 C-7
KROMMINGA, Folkert J. 1848–1905 C-11
Peter son of F.J. & T.P. d Sept. 6, 1897 1y 6m C-11
Tjede P. 1863–1953 C-11

LAHR, Carol W. 1914—C-22
Lahr Family Stone C-22
Val W. 1909–1978 C-22
LASHBROOK, three graves, no first names or dates C-21
LESTER "Family" no first names or dates S-23
LING, Fred J. Ohio Private. 158 Depot Brig WWI d June 25, 1936 S-14
LONG, Aiina D. mother d Feb 7, 1883. 53y 4m 1d S-4
LOOMIS, "Baby" no dates C-22
Earl Aug 21, 1901 Mar 17, 1946 C-22
LOPER, Ida May Jun 8, 1881 Oct 14, 1940 N-1
LOWE, Children of Asa Lowe no first names or dates S-24
LYONS, Mr. and Mrs. no dates S-9

MARQUAND, "Babies" Three babies, small stone, no dates C-14
Bert R. 1898–1968 C-14
Elias, D. father June 28, 1816–Nov 26, 1898 S-19
Ellsworth father 1861–1905 C-14
Family Stone S-20
Harriet L. June 3, 1847 Oct 10, 1864 17y 4m 7d S-19
Hattie Ann 1899–1968 C-14
Martha M. mother 1863–1907 C-14
Mary E. mother wife of E.D. May 30, 1821 Aug 3, 1899 S-19
Mother Marquand 1855–1930 C-14
Willmer E. Infant son of E.D. & M.E. Nov 7, 1863 Dec 24, 1863 S-19
McDONALD, Loese 1840–1904 S-7
McDonald, William 1829–1915 S-7
McELANEY, Alida L. wife 1846–1929 C-9
Andrew J. Private. CO B 15 Regt IL Inf Jan 13, 1840–Dec 8, 1933 C-9
Ann mother wife of George Oct 13, 1813 Jan 4, 1914 C-9
Family stone C-9
Julia A. 1868–1889 C-8
MEAD, E.W. 1859–1922 C-14
MILLER, Ambrose K. 1848–1872 S-17
MILLS, Faith Dec 31, 1957 daug of Rev and Mrs. K. Mills, Unity Presbyterian
    Church R.R.1 Clarksville S-19
MIX, Charles E. Co E 32 IA Inf WWI C-17
Mabel daug of A.H. & B.A. d Apr 2, 1862 1y 11m C-17
Rosa A. no dates stone broken C-17
MOCKFORD, Family Stone C-13
Harley son Sept 7, 1886 March 14, 1887 C-13
Matilda mother 1858–1940 C-13
Richard J. father Sept 21, 1856–Oct 8, 1910 C-13
MYERS, infant (no dates) S-3
Maud A. daug of C.T. & S. d Feb 18, 1877 3y 5d S-3

NASH, Lisle E. 1905–1936 C-16
NATION, Cora V. 1890–1973 S-8
Neal, Olive Mable d April 16, 1881 4y 2m 8d C-14
Thomas A. d Feb 3, 1890 38y 3m 17d C-14
W.L. Roy 1886–1946 C-18
NORTON, Edwin L. father 1838–1920 S-15
Family Stone S-15
Mary M. mother 1843–1929 S-15

OOSTER, Berend M.geb 4 Jan, 1895 gest 13 Oct 1918. "Christus ist mein Leben, Sterben ist mein Gewinn." ("Christ is my life death is my gain.") C-15
Family Stone C-15
Hinderina Sept 18, 1865–Sept 15, 1953 C-15
Rigt July 15, 1863–Aug 7, 1947 C-15
OSTER, Meint R. March 16, 1891–Aug 19, 1916 C-15

PADGETT, Infant (no dates) C-19
PATTERSON, Alonzo B.1851–1923 C-15
Family Stone C-15
Joseph d Jan 15, 1866 89y C-15
Mariah wife of William d Apr 25, 1889 76y 4m 28d C-15
Margaret May 3 to 30, 1892 C-15
Mary J. wife of W.H. 1843–1904 C-14
William d Oct 22, 1879 67y C-15
W.H. 1839–1902 C-14
PETERSEN, Harry Jr 1927–1984 C-14
PHILLIP, Albert Y. son of C.H & E d Mar 20, 1863 1m 4d S-17
POISAL, Almeda J. 1852–1919 S-17
Baby Sept 20, 1881 S-17
George H. 1876–1930 S-17
Hiram 1844–1934 CO G 32 Regt IA Inf Civil War S-17
Family Stone S-17
Myrtle 1882–1946 S-17
Sarah 1878–1879 S-17
POLK, Carl F. 1893–1965 C-17
Family Stone C 17
Merle 1892–1955 C-17
PRICE, Curtis E. son of E.B. & M.U. d Aug 6, 1863 2y 9m 2d C-17
Sarah J. wife of Cyrus J. d Dec 1, 1863 26y 1m 29d C-17

REYNOLDS, Byron H. (no dates) CO M 14 NY H A Civil War C-15
"Child" (no dates) C-15
RHODES, John no dates S-9
ROBBINS, Alzina wife of John S. d Dec 12, 1863 29y 8m 23d S-16

ROBINSON, Ellen mother wife of Ira no dates N-2
ROBERTS, Charles son of J.D. & M.D. Feb 9, 1879 1y 8m 6d C-3
Dorothy 1911–   C-6
Earl 1906–1966 C-6
Edward 1879–1963 C-6
Esther (infant) Dec 27, 1915–Feb 28, 1916 C-3
Family Stone C-3
Grant 1872–1954 C-3
Harlan A-son of William & Hester 1891–1911 C-6
Infant (no dates) C-6
J. Oliver father Mar 13, 1868–Jan 28, 1940 C-3
Jack H. 1939–1957 C-6
James D-1833–1915 CPL CO B 94 Regt IL Inf Civil War C-3
James David June 10, 1909 Sept 26, 1944 WWII C-3
Mae Barr mother Aug 1, 1885 Feb 9, 1958 C-3
Maria wife of J.D. 1835–1906 C-3
Myrtle 1883–1969 C-6
ROSS, no first name or dates S-23

SATTERLEE, three graves (no dates) S-7
SCHOON, Gertje geb 3 Dez 1841 gest 21 Mai 1922 C-13
Hilka 1872–1959 C-13
SCHOON, John B. geb 7 Mar. 1841 gest 9 Aug 1924 C-13
William 1874–1953 C-13
SCHOONMAKER, John W. son of N.T. 1850–1909 C-8
N.T. husband 1808–1889 C-8
Peter A. son of N.T. 1845–1901 C-8
Wife of N.T. 1826–1902 C-8
SHAFER, "Infant" no dates S-19
SHERBURNE, Alice L. 1881–1955 C-4
"Baby" no dates C-4
Family Stone C-4
Mary wife of H.G. D May 23, 1868 C-4
Wiley M. 1872–1954 C-4
SMITH, Alta E. 1883–1903 C-9
Darrel R. 1910–1981 C-12
Donald W. Apr 22, 1912 son of R.A. and L.V. C-12
Donovan R. Apr 22, 1912 son of R.A. and L.V. C-12
Elmer died 1886 C-9
Elmon died 1886 C-9
Hester A. 1876–1957 C-10
John R. 1880–1959 C-10
Lester R. 1893–1898 C-9
Lucy V. 1883–1959 C-12
Mary E. 1850–1920 C-9

Robert A. 1887–1960 C-12
William S. 1846–1928 C-9
SNYDER, Bethana mother Feb 27, 1816–Apr 8, 1864 S-6
Henry father Jan 29, 1815–Mar 9, 1897 S-6
Janet mother Feb 15, 1821–Feb 21, 1897 S-6
SPEARS, Eliza J. wife of Wm H. Feb 15, 1864 June 23, 1935 S-13
Homer 1892–1961 S-13
Ida May 1888–1960 S-13
William H. 1863–1939 S-13
SPENCE, Mack no dates S-17
SPIER, Pearl A. Walter 1887–1953 S-8
William 1883–1962 S-8
STEVENSON, John d July 11, 1876 88y 10m 18d C-2
Sarah d Apr 12, 1879 84y 1m 8d C-2
STORMS, George 1871–1943 C-3
STURDEVANT, Elizabeth A. 1899–1979 C-21
Family Stone C-21
James T. 1927–1928 C-21
Leon C. 1897–1975 PRIVATE US Army WWI C-21

TAMM, Eleanor R. 1921–   C-7
Roy C. Sept 1, 1913 Jan 13, 1980 parents of Larry and Marilyn Sgt. US Army
    WWII C-7
TAYLOR, John H.J. son of S.H. & Julia E. D Apr 21, 1863 2y 7m 9d C-18
THOMPSON, Lizzie M. wife of J.W. Oct 10, 1863 Apr 14, 1892 C-8
L.R. 1872–1925 C-21
Wilma daug of J.W. & L.M. Mar 24, 1888–Apr 14, 1888 C-8
Winifred H. 1872–1955 C-21
Family Stone C-8

VAN GUNDY David father Husband of S.A. D Jan 31, 1873 51y lm 9d Civil War Veteran
"Farewell my wife and children all, From you a father Christ doth call. Mourn not
    for me, it is in vain; To call me to your sight again." S-18
Family Stone S-18
Laura B. daug of D. & S.A. died July 22, 1881 17y 5m 20d S-18
Sarah A. mother d Feb 24, 1893 64y 5m 14d
"Farewell children, I am sleeping in the cold and silent grave, But my children cease
    to mourn me, though I rest beneath the sod for the gentle angels bear me to the
    bosom of our God." S-18
Wesley J. son of D. & S.A. died Sept 2, 1860 10y 7m 6d "This lovely bud, so young
    and fair called hence by early doom. Just came to show how sweet a flower, In
    paradise would bloom." S-18
VAN HAUREN, George H. Nov 20, 1932–Nov 25, 1932 C-12
Harm Jan 28, 1895 Jun 4, 1964 C-12
Mary Jungling Dec 30, 1902 July 24, 1964 C-12

VAN NEST, Eugene G. son of Olive R Van Nest Phipps Mar 16, 1929–June 5, 1942 C-3

WALTER, Bert 1875–1930 S-8
Elias O. father Jun 26, 1831–Jan 2, 1919 S-5
Rachel his wife Oct 28, 1832 Mar 28, 1891 S-5
WALTERS, Julius Apr 9, 1875 May 16, 1875 S-16
Mercy Jun 3, 1808 Dec 14, 1893 S-16
Servetus July 16, 1802 Mar 19, 1891 S-16
WATTERS, Clay L. 1883–1965 N-3
Family Stone N-3
Stella L. 1888–1966 N-3
WEBER, Ida no dates C-13
John no dates C-13
WHEELER, Anna 1884–1935 S-5
Roy 1882–1950 S-5
WHITEHEAD, Harvey (Peanuts) 1880–1970 S-8
WHITESIDE, Mary 1895–   C-5
Sam 1890–1960 C-5
WILCOX, David A. father 1869–1948 C-2
Eddie E. son of A.C.& B.E. died Aug 8, 1876 7m 8d C-3
WILCOX Elizabeth mother 1873–1925 C-2
Family Stone C-2
James D. 1902–1977 C-1
King D. 1900–1957 WWII Vet C-1
WILKENSEN, Beth L. 1904–   S-11
Dora E. 1882–1959 S-10
Edwin A. father CO L 15 Regt NY Inf Civil War Mar 20, 1847–July 20, 1933 S-10
Edwin V. 1899–1981 married 1925 parents of Harley J. and Shirley Jo S-11
Family Stone S-10 and S-11
Ida May mother 1856–1936 S-10
WILLIAMS, Delevan son of Wm & Rachel D Mar 5, 1859 3y 2d S-21
Family Stone S-21
Martha M. daug of Wm & Rachel D Jun 2, 1854 2 weeks S-21
William father d Aug 9, 1890 65y 1m S-21
WILSON, Forrest 1884–1953 C-10
Laura 1874–1948 C-10
WINCHELL, Infant (no dates) S-6
WOOD, Emma C. wife of John J. Died Sept 5, 1888 26y 10m 16d "My dearest friends that dwell above, I now have gone to see, All my friends in Christ below. Will soon come after me." S-18
WOODWARD, three stones, no first names or dates C-16
WOOLDRIDGE, Clarence W. (Duke) 1901–1938 S-1
David Lee 13 July, 1960 23 May, 1975 S-3
Donald E. 1910–1982 parents of Vylas, Darold, Marcy, Marvin S-1

Donna Lee 1945–2006
Florence M. 1879–1974 C-4
George W. 1876–1959 C-4
Ralph
Viola M. 1906–   S-1
WRIGHT, no first name or date S-11
WYGLE, Frank (Bud) 1911–1985 C-14

Unknown Graves

Infant, no name or dates (between Bowen and Robbins) S-16
Mr. and Mrs., no name or dates between Jaspers & Buss C-11
Infant, no name or dates (between Mix and Price) C-17
Three graves, no names or dates, between Hunt & Taylor C-18

OLD BRISTOW CEMETERY

The cemetery known as Old Bristow Cemetery can be found to the west of the small town of Bristow on County Road 33 in Section 24 of Pittsford Township. The cemetery has about forty graves, although it is believed that more burials exist. It is a well-kept cemetery, and efforts are being made to upright and mend those stones no longer standing properly.

Arnes, Leland son of W.G. & S.A. Arnes Sept. 14, 1902–Sept. 19, 1904 L47

Cass, Leffee S. wife. of H.H. Cass d Nov. 14, 1888 36y Ll3
Cass, Walter d Aug. 2, 1833 4m Ll3
Cass, Charles H. son of H.H. & L.S. Cass d? age? Ll3
Coonley, Earl son of C.T. & E.S. Coonley d Mar 20, 1883 10m 12d L27

Ellsworth, Little Charlie F. son of D.F. & M.E. Ellsworth d Aug. 2, 1875 2y 6m Ll5
Foote, J. Chester 1830–1905 L20
Foote, Jane T. 1828–1911 L20

Graham, May S. Mother 1854–1933 L32

Hatch, Arthur Garfield d Oct. 13, 1881 10m 24d L26
Hayes, two small stones in the southwest corner of the cemetery without markings on Lot 20 owned by Burt Hayes.
Hewitt, Thomas Apr. 19, 1888 89y 5m 15d Father L33
Hewitt, Sophia Mother Dec. 15, 1893 91y 5m 2d L33
Huber, Anna L. 1866–1942 L56

Ingles, Gordon son of O.P. & E.B. Ingels d July 1880 Ll4

Jackson, Willie H. son of J.H. & A.S. d 1880 age ? L28
Jakeway, Eva daug of R.I. & A. Jakeway Apr. 16, 1870 July 23, 1899 L35
Jones, Catherine M. 1830–1911 L56
Jones, Charles S. Co I 2nd Iowa Cav 1861–65 Civil War Vet Ll5
Jones, Charles L. 1835–1912 L56
Jones, Louise daug of E.A. & N. d May 5, 1898 Ll6
Jones, Tracy son of E.A. & N. no dates Ll6
Jones, E.A. 1860–1906 Ll6
Jones, Lonn E.M. son of F.A. & M.M. Jones d Dec. 29, 1821 ?y lm 29d L15
Jones, Frances A. July 24, 1832 June 22, 1902 Civil War Vet L15
Jones, Mary M. July 19, 1933–Apr. 24, 1926 L15

Miller, Clara E. daug of O.D. & F. Miller d July 2, 1886 2m 19d L29
Miller, O.D. Cor'l Co B 35th N.Y. Infantry Civil War Vet L29
Moots, Jane R. Mother 1837–1923 L48
Moots, John D. Father 1835–1915 L48
Moots, Angelica daug 1867–1888 L48
Moots, Martha A. daug 1872–1945 L48
Moots, Harvey R. son 1868–1946 L48

Royer, Ivah May daug of S. & G.A. d May 16, 1896 1y 3m 10d L45
Royer, Nina Fay daug of H.A. & M.M. d Feb. 27, 1897 1y 6d L45
Royer, W.W. Father d May 13, 1903 73y 10m 5d L25
Royer, Mary M. wife of W.W. Mother d Feb 6, 1888 56y L24

Sherman, Bob owner of L46 no stones
Sniffen, James J. son of D. & E. June 19, 1884–Feb 16, 1885 L34
Sniffen, David L. Father June 9, 1859–May 27, 1912 L34
Sniffen, Elizabeth A. Mother 1857–1930 L34

Tracy, A.D. June 11, 1826–Feb. 23, 1903 Father Ll7
Tracy, Horiatia M. Wife of A.D. July 21, 1829–Mar. 17, 1900 Ll7

Wallace, Lura C. Wife 1878–1946 L7
Wallace, John L. Husband 1872–   Spanish Am. War Vet L7

THE NEW ALBION CEMETERY

The New Albion Cemetery can be found in Section 33 of Jefferson
Township. The small settlement of New Albion once was located southeast
of the cemetery. People have told of another small burying ground south

of the platted town of New Albion. It was near an old mill that was found on land belonging to Ann Spain. Some stones and graves were said to have been moved to the New Albion Cemetery.

Harry and Earl Vanderlon and Jim and T.J. Spain once dug graves and were paid the sum of two dollars, to be split four ways. Memorial Day programs were held at the cemetery, usually the Sunday before Memorial Day. Once a twenty-five-acre grove of trees stood to the east of the cemetery. County workers would bring out planks to lay across stumps for seating. Children from Jefferson School No. 4, New Albion School and Albion School No. 5 brought fresh flowers and marched in the program. It has been said that the children who did not participate in the Memorial Day program would not receive report cards; thus, a large number of children attended.

In 2008, Paul Adelmund was sexton.

Burials

ADOLPHS, Lizzie 1894–1975 E-8
Adolphs, John 1890–1944 E-8
Adolphs, Martin 1916–1917, son of J. & L., E8

BENNETT, Laisilla W-2
Bennett, Harold L. 1900–1939 W-2
Bennett, Stuart J. 1934 67 yrs. W-2
Bennett, John B. W-2
BERLIN, Fredric 1820–1909 W-5
Berlin, Fredeika 1822–1910 W-5
Berlin, John 1863–1883 W-5
Berlin, Theresa 1838–1862 W-5
Berlin, Amalia W-5
Berlin, Adalia 1829–1856 W-5
BERTRAM, Hattie 1878–1957 E-8
Bertram, Fred 1875–1938 E-8
BIGSBY, Calista 1823–1862 W-2
BITNER, Dena Joe 1888–1913 W-3
BLAU, Grieise Tjebkes 1862–1907
Taken from WPA Records E-8
BRINKMAN, Katie 1863–1904 Mother E-7
Brinkman, Kobus 1855–1938 Father E-7
BROCKA, Mary 1882 21y 11m 4d Wife of E. E-5
BROWN, Simpson 1878 72y W-6
Brown, Phebe W-6
Brown, Mark S. 1874 ? W-6
BUSSE, Tillie M. 1936 Infant E-9

BUTTJER, Dirk 1851–1935 E-9
Buttjer, Wilhelmia 1860–1935 Parents of Kate Fleshner E-9

CARPENTER, Daniel 1827–1904 E-5
Carpenter, Henrietta 1883 87y 4m 12d Wife of G. E-5
Carpenter, Lucelia 1854–1921 E-5
Carpenter, Emma F. 1851–1929 W-2
Carpenter, Henry 1811–1885 W-2
Carpenter, James H. 1850–1922 W-2
Carpenter, Jimmy H. 1880–1881 W-2
Carpenter, Baby 1877 W-2
CHAPMAN, Little Eva 1865–1868 Daug. of H.E. & F.S. E-1
Chapman, Nancy F. 1869 65y Wife of Alpheus E-1
Chapman, Alpheus 1875 68y 5m E-1
Chapman, Charlie 1876 E-1
CHESLEY, L.D. 1869 32y 11m 6d E-2
CONN, Adam T. 1883 57y E-6
Conn, John T. 1899 48y E-6
Conn, Thomas E. 1867 78y 11m 23d E-5
Conn, Willie 1868–1876 8y 6m 16d Son of J.S. & E. E-6
Conn, Baby Daug. 1888 Daug. of W.W. & E. E-6
Conn, Charley 1865–1866 E-6
Conn, Robert H. 1829–1865 E-6
Conn, George 1863–1864 E-6
Conn, Joseph 1827–1899 E-6
Conn, Mary 1833–1879 E-6
Conn, Lizzie A. 1880 9y 11m 4d E-6
Conn, Eva Francis 1880 12y 11d E-6
Conn, Julia Mae 1880 10y 2m 2d E-6
Conn, Eva F. 1886 9m 7d E-6
Conn, Sarah Jane 1827-1913 86y E-6
CORDES, Grace 1906–1935 Wife & Mother E-9
Cordes, Anna 1865–1941 E-9
Cordes, Herman 1864–1945 E-9
Cordes, Johanna 1841–1921 W-2
Cordes, Fredrick B. 1839–1927 W-2
Cordes, Caroline 1875 W-2
COUCH, Almond 1851–1868 E-1
Couch, Hannah A. 1820–1896 E-1
Couch, Wilson 1819–1868 E-1
CRAMER, Carson 1891–1892 W-3

DAWSON, Catherine W. 1857–1866 E-6
Dawson, Catherine F. 1828–1887 Mother E-6
Dawson, Edward 1822–1904 Father E-6

Dawson, Fletcher F. 1868–1919 E-7
Dawson, John F. 1855–1856 E-6
Dawson, Margaret 1864–1913 E-7 1/2
Dawson, Rev. John 1819–1888 69y 4m 2d E-7
Dawson, Elizabeth 1888 72y 10m 2d Wife of Rev. John E-7
DEEM Monument W-5
DEWALL, Klaus 1863–1920 E-2
DOWNS, Augustine 1904 E-1
Downs, Ella A. 1866 7y 7m 17d Daug of M. & Al E-1
Downs, M. 1833 E-1
Downs, Ella E-1
Downs, Achsah 1904 Wife of M. E-1
DRING, John 1818–1895 W-4
Dring, Mother Eliza 1838–1913 W-4
Dring, George 1868–1926 W-4
Dring, Joseph 1871–1946 W-4

FLESHNER, Jacob E-8
Fleshner, Bessie M. 1905–   E-9
Fleshner, Kate 1879–1962 E-9
Fleshner, Stoffer 1877–1954 E-9
Fleshner, Philip E. 1895–1967 PRIVATE 163 Depot Brigade WWI E-9
Fleshner, Son of P.E. & B.M. E-9
Fleshner, Anna M. 1876–1905 Wife of Jacob E-8
Fleshner, George 1880–1915 E-8
Fleshner, Chris 1879–1965 E-8
Fleshner, Gertrude 1884–1927 Mother E-8
Fleshner, Clarence 1900–1953 E-8
Fleshner, Crtist H. 1897–1917 E-8
Fleshner, Infant 1917–1917 E-8
Fleshner, Gertie 1839–1899 Wife of C. E-7
Fleshner (Flessner) Christopher 1840–   E-7
FOURTNER, Mrs. Sarah W-9
GEERTSMAR, Swange 1899 E-2
GOODSETT, James R. 1872 1y 11m 16d W-2
Goodsett, William M. 1872 W-2

HALL, Joseph 1874 16y 8m Son of J. & M. E-4
HAYS, Rachel 1864 40y W-5
Hays, Susan 1848–1863 15y W-5
Hays, William 1826–1897 Unmarked W-5
HINDERS, Anna 1882–1966 E-9
Hinders, Ben 1865–1946 E-9
HOPLEY Monument E-6
HOVEY, Clara S. 1867 4y 8m 10d Daug. of L. & M. W-1

Hovey, Margia Ufford 1832–1900 W-1
Hovey, Lewis 1821–1877 46y 3m 2d W-1
HULSING, Geziena 1855–1893 Mother W-3
Hulsing Monument W-3
Hulsing, Ben 1857–1920 Father W-3
Hulsing, Lena 1888–1913 Unmarked W-3

IBLINGS, Alice 5y Daug. of Ubbe & Ella E-2

JOQUIS, Ellie W-3
Joquis, Fannie J. W-3
JRVINE, William 1872 Unmarked
JUNGLING, Hinderk 1892–1892 E-3

KELLY, John F. 3rd IA Batt. Civil War W-1
KENNEY (Kinney in WPA) Ede A. 1865 20y 10m 6d Wife of G.V. E-5
KETTWIG, Rolla 1901–1956 E-7
Kettwig, Annie (Anna) 1877–1903 Wife of J.C. E-7
KNAPP, Alfred B. 1807–1875 E-1
Knapp, Catharine 1867 61y 10m 14d E-1
KOPPLIN, Victor 1897 Son of J. & E. E-5
KOTHE, Louise Schweitzer 1807–1879 E-7
Kothe, James 1880–18-6 E-7
Kothe, Louise 1836–1912 Mother E-7
Kothe, Louis 1831–1909 Father E-7
Kothe, Edward 1875–1879 E-6
Kothe, Louise 1860–1864 E-6
Kothe, Emma 1858–1864 E-6
Kothe, William 1871–1874 E-6
Kothe, Fred D. 1855–1887 E-7
Kothe, Louise B. 1860–1947 E-7
KRAMER, Ella 1862–1914 W-3
Kramer, Ben 1863–1945 W-3
LINN, Andrew 1878 18y 10m 2d W-3
Linn, Florence M. 1884 18y 10m 2d W-3
Linn, Jenny Violet 1874 W-3
Linn, Baby W-3

MANZER, Nettie Mother E-3
Manzer, James A. 1845–1880 E-3
McCOY, C.W. 1873 Unmarked ?
McKEE, Melvin 1872 2y 10m 12d ?
MEAD, Emily S. 1864 24y 6m Wife of H.C. E-5
Mead, Celinda E. 1872 23y 19d W-2
MILLER, Peter K. 1878–1965 E-7

Miller, Gertie 1885–? E-7
Miller, Ralph J. 1909–1931 E-7
Miller, Ella E. 1851–1872 W-6
Miller, C.F.W. W-6
Miller, G.S.W. W-6
Miller, Father W-6
MUDLINGER, Clara Daug. of J.E. W-1

NAGEL, Mabel 1881 Daug. of J. & E. Kopplin E-5
Nagel, John H. 1822–1916 Father E-5
Nagel, Gerritdiena 1828–1881 Mother Wife of John H. E-5
Nagel, Martha 1861–1873 Daug. of J.H & G. E-5
Nagel, Embert 1827–1863 E-5
NIEMAN, Wiert W-9
Nieman, Leo W-9
Nieman, Mollie 1876 W-8
Nieman, Paul 1986 E-9
NORTH, Libbie C. 1845–1870 Unmarked W-7?

OLMSTEAD, Lilly Mae E-2
OSTENDORP, Greetje 1821–1906 E-2
OWEN, Aida J. 1865 4y 2m 20d Daug of L.D. & C. E-3
Owen, Esther E. 1866 21y 1m 3d Daug of L.D. & C. E-3
Owen, Caroline 1879 56y 9m 22d E-3
Owen, Lorenzo D. 1880 60y 22d E-3

PARKER, Mary 1866 E-6
Parker, Joseph E-6
Parker, Eliza 858 28y 1m E-6
PARRISH, Charley B. 1867 1y 13d Son of S. & M.L. E-5
PIERCE, Moses Co. F. 32nd IA Infantry E-5
Pierce, Harry 1875 21y 8m 1d Husband of F. E-5
Pierce, Oscar 1875 71y E-5
Pierce, Mary A. 1871 17y 8m 25d Wife of D.D. E-5
RUCHUELL, Sarah Unmarked W-3
RYKES, Eiso 1857–1907 E-3

SCHINITZER, Freddie Unmarked W-9
SCHNEIDER, J.D. 1867–1894 E-2
Schneider, Irene 1898–1915 Daug. of F. & A. E-2
SCHWEITZER, H.R. W-8
Schweitzer, W.F. W-8
Schweitzer, Katie W-8
Schweitzer, Louise Gross 1807–1879 E-7
SMITH, Gertie C. 1872 6y 9m W-4
STEENBERG, Johanna 1851–1928 Mother E-8

Steenberg, John 1844–1914 Father E-8
Steenberg, John 1884–1942 Son E-8
Steenberg, John 1850–1921 E-8
STEWART, Charles C. Co. 14th IA Infantry E-2
SWYGMAN, Arend 1905–1905 E-2
Swygman, Ella 1906–1907 E-2
Swygman, Zwaantje 1904–1914 E-2

TABOR, George W. W-5
Tabor, S.L. W-5
Tabor, Mother W-5
Tabor, Father W-5
THOMPSON, J.W. 1876 86y 6m 10d W-2
Thompson, Lyman A. 1867 W-2
Thompson, Artie 1844–1875 Wife of L.L. W-1
TIWMER, Jakob 1906–1906 Our Darling Baby E-1

VAN DEWSON, Mother W-5
Van Dewson, Calvin 1826–1881 W-5
Van Dewson, Frank 1865–1905 W-5
Van Dewson, Mercy 1840–1895 W-5
VANDERLON, Aaron W-9
Vanderlon, Reiko 1873–1942 E-7
Vanderlon, Emma 1884–1951 E-7
Vanderlon, Gertrude W-9
Vanderlon, Aaron W-9
Vanderlon, Albert 1881–1898 W-9
Vanderlon, John 1869–1890 W-9

WEEKS, Charlotte W-7
Weeks, Charles F. 1883 W-7
Weeks, Henry 1823–1898 Unmarked W-7
WELLEMS, William 1867–1931 Father E-8
Wellems, Wendelke 1864–1930 Mother E-8
Wellems, George 1897–1917 Son E-8
WETSELL, Dorcas 85y W-9
Wetsell, J.R. 1878 W-9
WILDEBOER, Harm 1876–1911 E-3
Wildeboer, Dave 1832–1887 E-3
Wildeboer, Mother 1832–1911 E-3
Wildeboer, Marie 1896–1920 E-3
WILLIS, Infant Son of F.H. & S. 1885 Buried with Nagels E-5

SOUTH VILMAR CEMETERY

St. John's Evangelical Lutheran Church of Vilmar owns three cemeteries. In 1882, an acre of ground was purchased from Fred Steer on land a half mile south of the church. This is the North Vilmar Cemetery. In 1885, a cemetery was started two miles west of the church in Section 14. This is South Vilmar Cemetery, or Folkers Cemetery. In November 1900, an acre of ground south of the church property was bought for seventy-five dollars from Mr. and Mrs. Henry L. Finke to be used for a second cemetery. The first burial in this cemetery was that of a seven-month-old child of Mr. and Mrs. Charles Tamm in May 1901 according to the *Centennial of St. John's Evangelical Church.*

The cemeteries were incorporated within the church in 1941. The first cemetery committee of three men was elected at the annual meeting in 1942. They were Conrad Senne, C.F. Wiebke and Henry F. Finke. The South Cemetery was enlarged in 1954 to the north toward the parsonage.

The South Vilmar Cemetery can be found in Section 3 of West Point Township.

Andrews, Ruth M. 1911–? L-99
Andrews, Clyde T. 1898–1968 L-99
Arjes, Dale 1935–1936 L-47
Arjes, Johann Votter July 11, 1855 Sept 1919 L-47
Arjes, Rentje Mutter Nov 16, 1861 Dec 5, 1944 L-47
Arjes. John C. 1885–1953 L-47

Baish, Ralph E. 1895–1984 L-52
Baish, Mrs. Ralph E. (Augusta L.) 1886–1964 L-52
Becker family stone L-10
Becker, Friedrich Vatter Apr 13, 1863–Oct 2, 1922 L-10
Becker, Mrs. Friedrich (Dorothea Kramer) Mar 16, 1873 Died Apr 8, 1911 Mutter
    L-10
Becker, Velma Mar 3, 1911 Apr 5, 1911 L-1
Benter, Charles 1892–1957 L-61
Benter, Mrs. Charles (Christina Wiegmann) 1892–1944 L-61
Benter, Wm. 1863–1942 L-32
Benter, Mrs. Wm. (Adeline Tamm) 1870–1949 L-32
Blaas, Emil 1899–1974 parents of Norma L-117 1/2
Blaas, Mrs. Emil (Milenda Kammeyer) 1903–1981 L-117½
Blaas, Fred 1872–1973 L-117
Blaas, Mrs. Fred (Emma Kraemer) 1878–1966 L-117
Blaas, William 1899–1979 parents of Dale L-118½
Blaas, Edna 1904–   L-118½

Bochmann, Christi Kay daug of M/M M.H. Aug 15, 1973 L-1
Bochmann, Henry J. 1882–1966 L-31
Bochmann, Mrs. Henry J. #1 (Minnie Salge) Oct 18, 1886–Feb. 10, 1911 L-31
Bochmann, Mrs. Henry J. #2 (Tona Franken) 1885–1962 L-31
Bochmann, Henry owner of L-15214
Brinkman, Henry D. June 19, 1866–Apr 23, 1953 L-7
Brinkman, Mrs. Henry D. (Caroline Koenig) Jan 12, 1870–Apr. 23, 1949 L-7
Brodrick, Baby L-45
Brodrick, Baby L-45
Brunner, Brenda Joyce daug of Orville and Lydia Jan 17–Feb 4, 1947 L-84
Brunner, Mrs. Orville (Lydia Constein) 1914–1984 L-84
Brunner, Orville D. 1919–   L-84
Buchholz, Carl C. 1875–1947 L-79½
Buchholz, Mrs. Carl C. (Sophie L. Kramer) 1876–1961 L-79½
Buchholz, Siegfied H. 1900–1949 L-8
Busse, Mutter Wilhelmine Nov 8, 1840–Oct 3, 1924 L-45
Busse, Votter Heinrich Jan 17, 1834 Oct 7, 1919 L-45
Busse, Mary L. 1863–1936 L-59
Busse, Frank W. 1859–1941
Busse, Mrs. Lena L-32½

Carr, Mrs. (Mable M. Tamm) 1908–1977 L-129
Carr, Joseph D. 1915–   L-129
Cassmann, Mrs. Melvin (Lucille Duane) 1929–1957 wife of Melvin L-113
Constien, Christoph Aug 29, 1852 Nov 13, 1933 Vater L-36
Constien, Mrs. Christoph (Catharena Stegen) wife of
Constien, Christoph Dec 7, 1857 Feb 22, 1904 L-36
Constien, George 1883–1950 L-97½
Constien, Mrs. George (Katharina Fick) 1889–1953 L-97½

DeBower, Ed H. 1896–1981 L-78
DeBower, Mrs. E. (Clara M. Paplow) 1902–1970 parents of Florence L-78
DeBower, John W. 1918–1976 L-149½
DeBower, Leona M. 1920–   parents of Russell, James and Kenneth L-149½
DeBower, Martin 1894–1971 L-138½
DeBower, Mrs. Martin (Frieda Heuer) 1896–1977 L-138½
Debner, Gertie 1912–?? L-115
Debner, Will H. 1905–?? parents of William, Kenneth, Wendell and Diane L-115
Debner, Kenneth owner of L-122
Debner, Will F. owner of L-123
Dralle, Erwin W. 1905–   L-76
Dralle, Velma L. 1905–   parents of Darold and Betty Jane L-76
Dralle, Lawrence C. 1914–   L-75
Dralle, Iris I. 1918–   L-75
Dralle, Paul H. 1912–   L-73

Dralle, Minerva A. 1914–   L-73

Dralle, Junior 1930–   1987 L-148

Dralle, LaVera S. 1933–   parents of Debra, Douglas Daniel and Doreen L-148

Dralle, Douglas H. June 28, 1958 Nov. 29, 1976 Father of Chad L-148

Dralle, Henry brother Aug 7, 1862 Mar 15, 1939

Dralle, Mrs. Henry (Charlotte Schmidt) Jan 9, 1867–Mar 25, 1921 L-19

Dralle, Henry 1890–1982 L-113½ 1336

Dralle, Mrs. Henry (Lottie Wessels) 1890–1968 L-113½

Dralle, Henry 1901–1979 L79

Dralle, Rosa 1904–   parents of Henry Jr. and Donna Mae L-79

Dralle, Mrs. Leo (Lorraine Kramer) 1922–1980 L-114

Dralle, Leo H. 1917–? parents of Barbara and Robert L-114

Dralle, Mrs. Paul (Dorothy L. Fick) 1914–1957 L-73

Dralle, Roger Dean 1936 L-19

Dralle, Sophia May 1, 1905–Sept. 25, 1905 L-19

Dralle, WM. C. 1871–1951 L-35½

Dralle, Mrs. Wm. C. (Lena Kammeyer) 1881–1957 L-35½

Dralle, Wm. H. Private Co M 352 Inf 88 Div WWI Jan 8, 1894–July 23, 1954 L-46½

Dralle, Herman 1910–   L-46

Dralle, Henrietta 1911–   parents of Roger and Leroy L-46

Dralle, Dale son of Anna and John Oct 28, 1935–Feb 28, 1936 L-47

Dukowitz, baby boy 1983–1983 Funeral Marker L-157

Edeker, Edna 1915–   L-94

Edeker, Clarence 1911–1972 L-94

Edeker, Henry 1880–1956 L-97

Edeker, Mrs. Henry (Anna Fick) 1882–1959 L-97

Edeker, Herman 1904–1952 L-95

Edeker, Mrs. Herman (Minnie Rodenbeck) 1904–1965 L-95

Edeker, Mary no dates daug of Wm. and Emma L-6

Ellerman, Henry 1892–1976 L-118

Ellerman, Mrs. Henry (Adaline Fick) 1893–1970 L-11

Ernsting, Conrad 1872–1953 L-91

Fick, Charles 1884–1953 L-38

Fick, Mrs. Charles (Minnie Busse) 1889–1959 L-38

Fick, Peter Geb 18 Dez 1848 Gest 21 Juli 1901 Vater L-12

Fick, Velma daug of C. & M. Nov 20, 1909 L-38

Fick, Marie nee Henken Nov 24, 1859 June 4, 1942 L-12

Fick, Wilhelm C. Nov 21, 1891–Jan 10, 1919 L-46½

Finke, Baby Leslie L-81

Finke, Cheryl Kay daug of Fred and Beverly Sept 6, 1955 L-88

Finke, Fred W. 1911–1976 Msgt US Army WWII L-88

Finke, Beverly B. 1929–1968 L-88

Finke, Henry H. 1891–1969 L-116

Finke, Mrs. Henry H. (Sophia Becker) 1894–1980 L-116

Finke, John J. 1896–   L-18

Finke, Louise Feb 7, 1904–May 28, 1904 Child of H.L. & M. Finke L-18

Finke, Robert Oct 7–8, 1946 son of Henrietta and Lawrence L-81

Finke, Infant son Nov 30, 1903 L-18

Folkerts, Folkert 1886–1953 Husband L-55

Folkerts, Mrs. Folkert (Wilhelmine Dralle) 1888–1920 wife of Folkert L-55

Franken, Emma 1904–1959 L-83

Franken, Frieda H. 1900–1953 L-83

Franken, Mrs. Jacob #2 (Anna VanHorn) 1873–1957 L-83

Franken, Jan Mar 30, 1887–June 16, 1929 L-68

Franken, Mrs. Jan (Grace Stopplemoor) 1898–1937 Funeral Marker L-68

Franken, Wilbur H. Iowa SO USNR WWI June 26, 1925–Apr 27, 1954 L-68

Franken, Bernard owner of L-121½

Hagemann, Fred R. 1871–1924 L-1

Hagemann, Mina L. no dates L-1

Hencken, Carl 1856–1943 Father L-93½

Hencken, Mrs. Carl (Wilhelmina Becker) 1855–1937 Mother L-93½

Hencken, Chris 1887–1975 L-93½

Hencken, Mrs. Chris (Minnie Rover) 1889–1965

Henning, Joshua Charles Apr 24–25, 1981 son of Dennis and Carol L-153

Heuer, Edward 1879–1928 Father L-66

Heuer, Mrs. Edward (Minnie Schraqe) 1883–1963 Mother L-66

Heuer, John 1894–1971 L-116½

Heuer, Johanna 1897–   L-116½

Heuer, William 1869–1936 L-67

Heuer, Mrs. William (Anna Kroemer) 1874–1938 L67

Heuer, William H. 1905–1967 L-80

Heuer, Ida C. 1977–1985 L-80

Hilmer, Peter H.C. May 14, 1828–Jan 5, 1921 L-52

Hilmer, Mrs. Peter H.C. (Katharine D.) Oct 31, 1827–Oct 27, 1915 L-52

Heuer, Alfred owner of L-169

Heuer, Jack, Dr. Ralph W. 1900–1974 L-136

Heuer, Dorothy M. 1905–1987 L-136

Jakel, Charlotte 1909–1936 L-25

Jakel, Conrad 1862–1943 L-25

Jakel, Mrs. Conrad (Sophie Brockmeyer) 1867–1933 L-25

Jakel, Elmer Apr 30, 1911–Apr 15, 1912 L-25

Jakel, Wilhelm Jan 8, 1891–Jan 16, 1913 L-25

Jakel, Charlotte 1868–1902 L-25

Kammeyer, Carl 1874–1959 L-51

Kammeyer, Mrs. Carl (Emma Reinking) 1878–1970 L-51

Kammeyer, Elve 1916–1919 L-51

Kammeyer, Elven 1912–1914 L-51

Kammeyer, Henry 1862–1938 L-49

Kammeyer, Mrs. Henry (Eleanora) 1868–1962 L-49

Kammeyer, Vern 1906–1921 L-17

Kammeyer, Wilhelm 1870–1923 L-17

Kammeyer, John 1898–1987 L-17

Kammeyer, Mrs. Wilhelm (Martha Schroeder) 1878–1965 L-17

Klunder, Mrs. Otto (Frieda Kroemer) 1904–1947 L-69

Klunder, Lydia 1909–1985 L-69

Klunder, Otto 1904–   L-6

Koester, Herman T. Dee 31, 1880–May l0, 1957 L-135

Koester, Mrs. Herman (Caroline Voights) Sept 7, 1889 Mar 22, 1959 L-135

Kollmann, Herman 1878–1971 L-44

Kollmann, Mrs. Herman (Minnie Wedeking) 1883–1962 L-40

Kollmann, Valeda 1910 L-40

Kollmann, John 1884–1975 L-125½

Kollmann, Mrs. John (Sophia Hencken) 1885–1974 L-125½

Koneg, Baby no dates L-1

Kramer, Christine 1880–1949 L-8

Kramer, Fred J. 1898–1983 L-9½

Kramer, Mrs. Fred J. (Emma Rover) 1901–1984 parents of Loraine, Kathleen and Edna

Kramer, Friedrick Vater May 13, 1841 May 29, 1913 L-8

Kramer, Mrs. Friedrick (Christina Engelmahl) Mutter May 2, 1842–May 15, 1916 L-8

Kramer, Julia Marie 1938 daug of Kurt and Nellie L-8

Kramer, William 1871–1964 L-9

Kramer, Mrs. William (Tatje Reents) 1875–1969 L-9

Kroemer, Henry J. Nov 26, 1880–Aug 25, 1925 L-65

Kroemer, Mrs. Henry J. (Ella L. Schrage) Dec 13, 1889 Apr 17, 1972 L-65

Kruse, Carl 1897–1980 L-74

Kruse, Minnie 1903–   parents of Charles and Shirley L-74

Kruse, Frank C. 1909–   L-133

Kruse, Mildred M. 1913–   parents of Gary and Janet L-133

Kruse, Herman A. 1893–   L-139

Kruse, Anna c. 1895–   parents of Verlin, Edward and Louis Ann L-139

Kruse, Anna 1897–1904 daug L-23

Kruse, Christian June 14, 1857 Aug 16, 1911 Vater L-3

Kruse, Mrs. Christian (Auguste Ziemke) 1867–1914 Mutter L-3

Kruse Emil F. 1922–1923 L-50

Kruse, Fred C. l895–1978 L-50

Kruse, Mrs. Fred C. (Cena L. Workman) 1898–1977 L-50

Kruse, Henry 1901–l985 L-23

Kruse, Herman 1865–1940 Father L-23

Kruse, Mrs. Herman (Anna Niehaus) Mother L-23

Kruse, John F. 1956–1979 Father of Andrew
Kruse, Rena C. 1929–   L-l6
Kruse, Eldo C. 1926–   L-l62
Kruse, Leo 1902–1976 L-3
Kruse, Lillie C. 1905–1906 daug L-23
Kruse, Lillie no dates L-23
Kruse, Wilhelm Apr 22, 1903–May 15, 1979
Kruse, Pauline no dates L-23

Lampman, Frieda wife of Alfred L-124
Lampman, Alfred 1916–   L-124
Lampman, Mrs. Alfred (Lillian Salge) L-124
Lampman, Frederick A. son of Alfred and Frieda June 21, 1962 L-124
Lienemann, Harm 1872–1946 Father L-60
Lienemann, Mrs. Harm (Jankten) 1878–1931 Mother L-60
Lienemann, Trientje "Tena" 1915–1927 L-60

Marlette, Vernon 1911–1971 L-55
Marlette, Lillian 1914–   L-55
Menken, Ricklef 1903–1984 L-141
Menken, Evelyn 1918–   parents of John, Thomas, Mari Ann and Kathryn L-141
Meyer, Wilhelm July 29, 1863–Apr 23, 1948 Father L-85
Meyer, Mrs. Wilhelm (Anna Polakova) Nov 25, 1883–Jan 2, 1978 Mother L-85
Miller, Edward Brother 1906–1986 L-171
Miller, Henry F. 1904–1976 L-72
Miller, Mrs. Henry F. (Grace M.) 1912–1965 parents of Lynn and Darrell L-72
Miller, Marcia d 1939 L-72
Miller, Minnie Apr 16, 1897–Sept 9, 1969 L-6
Miller, Paul d 1936 L-72
Miller, Wilhelm Nov 13, 1870–Mar 22, 1944 L-6
Miller, Mrs. Wilhelm (Minnie Koenig) Oct 18, 1872 Mar 16, 1954 L-6
Miller, Will C. 1895–1973 L-129½
Miller, Mrs. Will C. (Anna L) 1900–1978 L-129½
Miller, Edward owner of L-119

Niehaus, Anna L. June 16, 1908 Nov 16, 1969 L-104
Niehaus, Herman 1883–1960 L-9
Niehaus, Mrs. Herman (Wilhelmina Wiebke) 1888–1953 L-9
Niehaus, Herman W. June 28, 1910–Nov 24, 1959 L-90
Niehaus, John Apr 3, 1870–Aug 19, 1988 L-90
Niehaus, Mrs. John (Charlotte Schrage) Dec 29, 1880–July 2, 1959 L-90
Niehaus, Leona M. May l, 1917–May 4, 1917 daug L-35
Niehaus, William Feb 12, 1890–Nov 21, 1944 L-35
Niehaus, Mrs. William (Hulda Rover) Feb 26, 1888–Feb 28, 1969 L-35
Niehaus, Mary, daug 1896–1985 L-24
Niehaus, Herman Father 1863–1929 L-24
Niehaus, Mina Mother 1865–1955 L-24

Paplow, Henry W. Feb 23, 1880 Feb 16, 1941 L-79
Paplow, Mrs. Henry W. (Mathilda Constien) Sept 10, 1898 Aug 1, 1952 L-79
Popinga, Marie C. Miller Oct 14, 1900–Oct 4, 1927 L-6
Poppe, Ewald 1893–1963 L-125
Poppe, Mrs. Ewald (Mary Schmidt) 1896–1979 L-125
Prange, Clifford 1920–1921 son of F. & A. L-57
Prange, Conrad, 1877–1930 L-57
Prange, Mrs. Conrad (Sophie Edeker) 1897–1962 L-57
Prange, Earnest H. 1883–1969 L-86
Prange, Mrs. Earnest H. (Sophia Wiegmann) 1883–1976 L-86
Prange, Fred 1889–1967 L-56
Prange, Alma 1890–1985 L-56
Prange, Lawrence 1908–1965 L-?
Prange, Leland 1926 son of F. & A. L-56
Prange, Verland 1930 son of F. & A. L-56
Prange, Willie F. Iowa Private Infantry WWII Feb 25, 1924–Feb 6, 1945 L-86

Riggert, Christoph H. Jan 1, 1891 May 30, 1939 L-44
Riggert, Mrs. Christoph H. (Lousie Voights) Dec 17, 1893–Dec 21, 1973 L-44
Riggert, Nolda Marie Apr 30, 1916 May 12, 1923 L-44
Rodenbeck, Wilhelm Father Jan 30, 1875 Apr 16, 1914 L-26
Rodenbeck, Mrs. Wilhelm (Sophia Dralle) Mother June 2,1877–May 30, 1911 L-26
Rodenbeck, William C. 1899–1983 L-27
Roork, Elv owner of L-160
Roose, Stanley owner of L-120

Salge, Minna Louise d Feb 12, 1933 L-1
Salge, Conrad 1891–1960 L-4
Salge, Mrs. Conrad (Lena Busse) 1896-1973 parents of Lillian and Eugene L-4
Salge, Fred H. 1893–1984 L-33
Salge, Mrs. Fred H. (Ella Busse) 1894-1967 L-33
Salge, Fred Sr. 1858–1951 Father L30
Salge, Baby no dates L-30
Salge, Mrs. Fred Sr. (Sophie) 1867–1950 Mother L-30
Salge, Ida 1899–   L-43
Salge, Henry 1898–1968 L-43
Salge, Glenn F- 1919–1970 L-33
Salge, Infant son of M/M F. Salge Sr. no date
Salge, Verne son of H. & I. Apr 16, 1919–Mar 14, l920 L-43
Salge, Wm. L. 1895–1966 parents of Darlene, Minna, Shirley and Donald L-2
Salge, Mrs. Wm. L. (Minnie C. Finke) 1899–1968 L-2
Schmidt, Conrak 1859–1927 L-13
Schmidt, Mrs. Conrad (Minnie Fick) 1879–1955 L-13
Schoeneman, Russell D. Iowa Tec 5 Co E 22nd Inf Rigt WWII L-127

Schoeneman, Rusty Dean Oct 14, 1974 L-127
Schoeneman, Burdella 1916– 1-127
Schrage, August 1868–1964 L-5
Schrage, Mrs. August (Augusta Kramer) 1878–1956 L-5
Schrage, Boto 1905–1974 L-128
Schrage, Lela 1906– L-128
Schrage, Carl June 12, 1888 Oct 27, 1964 L-48
Schrage, Mrs. Carl #1 (Ida Kammeyer) Nov 21, 1887 May 10, 1915 L-48
Schrage, Mrs. Carl #2 (Minnie Wiegman) Aug 4, 1886 June 28, 1945 L-48
Schrage, Clarence A Jan 11, 1911 July 27, 1962 L-126
Schrage, Valda M. May 20, 1913– parents of Edwin and Linus L-126
Schrage, Ed A Sept 7, 189–Jan 31, 1920 L-20
Schrage, Mrs. Eldo (Laura M. Paplow) 1914–1968 L-169
Schrage, Lamb stone no writing L-5
Schrage, Eldo E. 1911– parents of Carol Marie L-168
Schrage, Ferdinand 1897–1904 L-5
Schrage, Frida 1896 L-5
Schrage, Hermine E. 1890–1974 L-63
Schrage, Ernest W. 1891–1960 parents of Eugene, Viola, Edith Ann, Robert and Lester L-63
Schrage, Sophie Oct 13, 1888–July 29, 1944 L-62
Schrage, William Oct 19, 1885–Mar 23, 1948 parents of Clarence and Burdella L-62
Schrage, F.W. Oct 9, 1893 Oct 22, 1918 Vet in Hericurt, France Corp Co A 352 Inf L-20
Schrage, Galen H. d 1936 son of A. & N. Schrage L-71
Schrage, Henry 1855–1937 Father L-21
Schrage, Mrs. Henry (Louise Schmidt) 1861–1945 Mother L-21
Schrage, Joan M. 1939–1940 daug of A. & N. Schrage L-11
Schrage, William Apr 5, 1857 Apr 8, 1938 L-20
Schrage, Mrs. William (Louise Reinking) Nov 7, 1863–Apr 21, 1934 L-20
Schueler, August F. 1893–1961 L-4½

Schueler, Minnie A. 1898– parents of Elizabeth and August Jr. L-4½
Steer, Ernest 1884–1950 L-98
Steer, Mrs. Ernest (Augusta Fick) 1895–1979 L-98
Steer, Leonard H. 1911–1972 L-137½
Stemmerman, Edward 1891–1970 WWI L-138
Stemmerman, Mrs. Edward (Sophia Finke) 1894–1978 L-138
Struckmeyer (Julia Hencken Wiegman) 1889–1961 L-64
Seehusen, George owner of L-146

Tamm, Charles, 1874–1950 L-14
Tamm, Mrs. Charles (Alvina) 1873–1948 L-14
Tamm, Friedrich A 1901 L-14

Tanderup, Heinrich 1840–1906 L-42

Tanderup, John 1873–1957 Funeral Marker L-42

Tiedens, Mrs. (Hermine Franken) 1902–1959 L-83

True, Lloyd J. 1903–1964 L-87

True, Mrs. Lloyd J. (Alvina M. Prange) 1904–1983 L-87

Voights, Vern 1918–1985 L-41

Voights, Carl H. Oct 2, 1875–Mar 10, 1954 L-82

Voights, Mrs. Carl H. (Emma Niehaus) Nov 12, 1876–Apr 6, 1954 L-82

Voights, Clarence C. Iowa Cp1 Field Artillery WWII Sept 20, 1915–Nov 12, 1947 L-91½

Voights, Dick 1891–1956 L-39

Voights, Mrs. Dick (Mary Koester) 1886–1946 L-39

Voights, Eldo 1914–1971 L-135

Voights, Violet 1915–   L-135

Voights, Elmer Son July 9–Dee 26, 1910 L-41

Voights, Fred H. 1905–1979 L-152

Voights, Luella E. 1909–   parents of Larry L-152

Voights, Henry 1882–1953 L-16

Voights, Mrs. Henry #1 (Louise Schrage) 1883–1913 L-16

Voights, Mrs. Henry #2 (Minnie Schrage) 1892–1981 L-16

Voights, Henry J. 1909–1975 L-151

Voights, Huelda L. 1910–L151

Voights, Herman Dec 17, 1908–? 8, 1909 L-39

Voights, Baby no dates L-39

Voights, Herman Father Sept 22, 1884–Dec 6, 1971 L-41

Voights, Mrs. Herman (Mary Conrad) Mother July 30, 1883 Sept 11, 1955 L-41

Voights, Leona 1913–1914 L-16

Voights, Vern 1918–1985 L-16

Voights, Linda d Oct 14, 1934 L-89

Voights, Merlyn 1920–1977 L-142

Voights, Susie 1920–   parents of Susanne, Bruce, Brenda and Kevin L-142

Voights, Kenneth 1913–1986 L-143

Voights, Caryl 1916–   parents of David and Keith L-143

Voights, Leroy owner of L-141½

Voights, David-owner of L-143½

Wagner, Larry owner of L-77½

Waller, Marvin A. son July 26, 1912 Mar 11, 1913 L-29

Waller, Herman W. Jr. 1908–1961 L-29

Waller, Herman Sr. Aug 28, 1881–Mar 5, 1950 L-29

Waller, Mrs. Herman Sr. (Wilhelmine Voights) Mar 12, 1880–May 12, 1962 L-29

Weber, Leanard J. owner of L-100

Weinberg, Bernice 1921 daug of Wm. and Alvena L.

Weinberg, Fredrick Oct 16, 1836–Feb 9, 1914 Father L-15
Weinberg, Mrs. Fredrick (Margrata) Apr 13, 1843–Mar 15, 1915 Mother L-15
Weltner, Margaretha Sept 2, 1838–Nov 11, 1901 L-28
Weltner, Martin Nov 20, 1932–May 12, 1913 L-28
Wiebke, Carl 1856–1941 Father L-34
Wiebke, Mrs. Carl (Charlotte Debner) 1859–1916 Mother L-34
Wiebke, Charles F. Father Apr 13, 1891–June 22, 1974 L-53
Wiebke, Clara daug of C.H. & Minnie July 1, 1903–Sept 1, 1905 L-53
Wiebke, Mrs. Charles F. (Bauwina C. Franken) Mother Jan 12, 1898–Sept 22, 1962 L-53
Wiebke, Helen B. 1922–   L-157
Wiebke, Willard B. 1917–   parents of Ronald and Rynonda L-157
Wiebke, Floyd son of C. & B. Jan 31–Mar 11, 1920 L-53
Wiebke, Frederick 1896–1977 L-158
Wiebke, Dorthea 1899–   parents of Roy L-158
Wiebke, Henry 1886–1962 L-58
Wiebke, Mrs. Henry (Antje Franken) 1892–1976 L-58
Wiebke, Infant daug of C. & B. Mar 15, 1921 L-159
Wiebke, William 1893–1975 L-159
Wiebke, Mrs. William (Elsie Bochmann) 1896–1980 parents of Orville, Gale and Fern L-159
Wiebke, Orville owner of L-160
Wiegmann, Baby no date
Wiegmann, Conrad C. 1891–1953 L-93
Wiegmann, Mrs. Conrad C. (Ida True) 1895–1969 L-93
Wiegmann, Duane Michael Sept 20, 1952 son of Evelyn and Orville L-96
Wiegmann, Orville "Mike" 1923-1986 Korea L-96
Wiegmann, Evelyn I. 1927–   parents of Duane, Diane and Dennis L-96
Wiegmann, Frank 1900–1981 L-21
Wiegmann, Frieda 1909–   parents of Gloria and Marolyn L-21
Wiegmann, Heinrich 1886–1919 L-54

Wiegmann, Julia 1889–1961 L-54
Wiegmann, Elsie L. 1919–   L-54
Wiegmann, Christ H. 1911–   L-54
Wiegmann, Infant daug of C.C. & Ida Aug 19, 1915 L-18
Wiegmann, Glenn H. owner of L-179
Wix, Baby no dates L-3
Wix, Frederick Vater Mar 6, 1964–Dec 27, 1923 L-37
Wix, Maria born Mueller Jan 17, 1874–Mar 14, 1907 L-37
Wix, Mrs. Frederick (Mina Coors) 1870–1953 Mother L-37
Wubbena, Miko 1909–1938 son L-70
Wubbena, Mike 1880–1947 L-70
Wubbena, Mrs. Miko (Louise Koenig) 1884–1933 L-70

Lamb, stone no dates found between Tamm and Cassmann. This could possibly be the seven-month-old child of M/M Charles Tamm who died in 1901 and was the first burial in this cemetery.

WEST POINT CEMETERY

Although the West Point Cemetery is found in Jackson Township, Section 30 of Bremer County, it has been added because of its closeness to the Butler County line. The cemetery is located two miles east of Shell Rock and three and a quarter miles south, only one mile into the next county. Since families from Butler County buried their kin in the nearest cemetery and the West Point Cemetery was the only burying grounds this close to the county border, undoubtedly many of Butler County's citizens were buried in this small cemetery. The West Point Cemetery is on a hill about four miles west of Janesville.

The land for the cemetery was purchased for five dollars from Isaac West on October 10, 1863, by the Union Ground Burying Society. The cemetery was known as the Waverly Junction Cemetery. The cemetery was neglected until May 22, 1922, when a group of neighbors and friends formed a cemetery organization. They cleaned it up, planted perennials and changed the name to West Point Cemetery, according to the *Bremer County Cemetery Records*.

West Point Cemetery, Waverly Junction, Iowa. *Taken by Sherri Willey, 2008, used with her permission.*

Walt Ruth currently marks the graves and oversees the cemetery.

ADAMSON, Rachel wife of A.J.
Andrew J. 10-27-1869 51y 10m 6d
AKREND, John B. 1-29-1874 1y
Mary wife of John 1-8-1882 60y 4m
Mary J. 1-29-1886 18y 3m 5D daug of J. & M.

BENTON, Thomas
Samuel B. 3-1805 5-1872
Margaret 6-1814 12-1890
Phoebes 12-1840 3-1871
BOOTS, Nelson R. 1-29-1873 33y G.A.R.

BRIDEN, W.H. (Orrin) no date
Ricky D. 1951–
BROWN, Dan 11-6-1877 70Y 10m 8d
Harry 10-23-1867 3 weeks 8d
BURKE, David C. 3-5-1835 8-6-1896 Civil War Veteran
Mary E. 4-17-1868 6-7-1837
Margaret 9-5-1868 5-2-1958
Charles 11-1-1871 2-2-1946
Harriet 7-26-1843 1-11-1895
C.L. 1899–1907
Eugene W. 1873–1968
Margaret M. 1884–1958
Hattie E. 1880–1958

CALHOUN, L. no dates
CHASE, Mrs. Bert no dates
CLEMENTS, Betsy E. 1849–1939
Albert 1851–1918
Wife of Albert d 1938
COLBURN, infant daug L.M. 1922
COTTON, Lydia A. 2-8-1852 12-27-1892
CROWELL, Wilbur B. 1876–5-23-1928
Ella C. 1872–1935
Wilbur G.A.R.

DAVIS, Fred M. 1868–1888
Verna Adams 1867–1938
DEAN, Maudie 1886–1888
Margaret 1866–1898
DEWEY, Cynthia 1816–1893
Father 1816–
Edward no date
George 1819 Mass. 1-20-1884
Dewey, Cassandra Hooper wife of George 4-16-1894 71Y 7d
Richard no date
DIX, Harvey 1897–1968
Mabel E. 1912–1976
DOVE, Walter (W. & L.) 2m
DRYER, George E. son of J.W. & S. 6-16-1857 12y 6m 26d
Sally W. 1811–1877
John W. 1807–1875
Two children of J. & S. age 20 & 28

EDWARDS, Elizabeth 5-22-1872 29y
George infant son of W. & E. 8-16-1918

GIFFIN, T.S. 12-14-1879 31Y lm 4d
Jane 1789 9-12-1853 Wife J.
Henry W. 1857–1866
Enna J. 5-3-1862 5y 4m 5d daug of H. & L.
Jefferson C. 12-19-1861 6y 8m son of T. & E. J.
Levina C. 1859 5-18-1853 daug of T. & E. J.
GLENDON, Reid no date
GRAY, Hazel Emma 5-12-1903 7-26-1908

HAMILTON, George W. 7-4-1851 3-15-1921
Rosina E. 5-5-1854 to 3-7-1936
Elnah M. 1883–1901
HANSEN, Fred no date
Ida A. 6-4-1868 to 3-2-1908
HURLEY, Emma E. 1-17-1878 20y

JACOBS, Clara 5-31-1882 33y 3m 23d
JAMES, Irene no date
E. 2-26-1915 9-19-1947
JARCHOW, Hazel 1900–
Walter H. 1897–1979
Merel Edward 1932–
JOHNSON, Mary 6-11-1878 59y

KELLER, Anna J. 1871–1950
Charles F. 1863–1922
Ella 12-30-1857 11-9-1935
KINZER, Ed no date
KIRKPATRICK, Mr. & Mrs. no date
Ella 12-30-1857 9-9-1935
Ja 2-4-1855 to 12-17-1935

LOCKWOOD, Samuel no date

MANN, Amelia 1861–1888
McCAFFREE, Lovisa R. 8-17-1850 5-28-1932
W. Hardin 6-11-1849 4 to 2-4-1930 third white child born in Bremer County
Ruth L. 1-22-1918 2-11-1918
Nellie M. 1879–1959
Hannah A. 1875–1950
Walter 10-26-1881 to 2-13-1927 son of W.H. & J. Meyer
William Paul 1905–1906

MEDDERS, Aaron 11-30-1816 to 9-18-1894
Anna 1874 5-29-1898 wife of Frank
Edna M. Clemments wife of Abner 1876 4-2-1906
Hannah 1844–1927
Mary M. 4-9-1888 15y 4m 3d daug of S. & H.
George William 1866 to 12-6-1870
George Ed 1879–1971
Frank 5-19-1895 24y
Lenora 1879–1963
Frank 1874–1942
Samuel no date
Abner 1858 to 4-12-1937 b Nashua d Plentywood, Mont.
McMANUS, James 179?–186?
MURLEY, Emma L. 6-17-1878(?) 20y 6m 15d
MEYERS, Hettie A. 184?–8-4-1890

O'BYE John V. 9-12-187? 18y 12m 12d
ORVIS, Jessie E. 1878–1941
OLMSTEAD, Electa 6-2-1877 42y 4m 18d
George S. ???–16-1866

PALMER, Althea Powell wife of Ernie 1901
Ruth S. 4-12-1830 to 2-5-1892
S. 2-12-1821 to 7-7-1903
Eugene S. 9-16-1860 to 1-26-1914
Martha 4-14-1862 to 10-10-1942
Elmer C. 1855–1923
Lydia J. 1836–1915
POWERS, Etta M. 1863–1923

QUEEN, Hiram Civil War CO B 38th Iowa Inf

RAGSDALE, James E
Laura B. 1891–1972
Sp. William S. 1891–1978
Baby 1976
RICH, no names or dates
RIPPBERGER, Mrs. Verna 1888 2–1923
child Mae, Ruth, Lila and Cleo
RUSH, Harry D. 10-13-1868 5y 6m
Alexis 1832–1901
Maria 1839–1915
Jessie no dates
Elias no dates
RUSSELL, William Civil War Veteran 12-25-1833 to 10-27-1906

RESSIER, Laura 1847–1916

SAILOR, William b Monrow Co. Ohio 7-22-1818 to 9-15-1896
Fannie Rush 5-29-1820 7-17-1899 Mother of Mrs. J. McCaffree, Mrs. W.H. McCaffree, Mrs. J. Pitts
Aaron 11-17-1867 28y 2m 8d
SHERBURNE, Adella wife of W.H. 10-19-1846 to 4-17-1907
W.H. 4-19-1834 to 5-30-1812
Cora E. 8-6-1879 to 8-16-1881
SHORES, Mary S. Dewey 10-7-1896 34y 8m 28d
Johnathan Martin husband of Mary Dewey 10-7-1839 to 10-17-1920 b Oxford Twp. Guernsey Co. Ohio
Maurice Ray 12-15-1874 to 4-18-1898
STANNARD, Phares C. 1876–1946
Myrtie A. 1882–1968
STOUT, G. no date

TEMPLEMAN, Dorothy Alene 6-13-1903 to 1-31-1978
Lewis F. 3-23-1898 to 7-14-1980 Pfc. US Army WWI
TURNER, James L. 1904–1969
Mable 1910–1947
Infant son

VEZA William H. Civil War Veteran CO G 9th Iowa Cav
VOSSBERG, Fred W. 1888–1968
Carrie 1890–1921

WEST, Myers Ed no date
Isaac 1797 to 3-10-1877
WIGHTMAN, Eliza 1813 to 7-28-1868
Franklin G. 1803 to 5-29-1881
Child male
E.N. 4-14-1832 to 11-1-1906 wife of Geo E.
George E. 8-5-1833 to 1-21-1916

WILL, Kathe 1905–
Max 1895–1977
WING, Phoebe S. 12-1840 3-1871 daug of S. & M. Benton
WRIGHT, Sam no dates

Bibliography

Aredale Centennial Book. N.p.: 2000.

Atlas of Butler County, Iowa. Mason City, IA: Anderson Publishing Co., 1917.

Bremer County Cemetery Records. N.p.: Bremer County Genealogical Society, 1983.

Bremer County 150ᵗʰ Anniversary Celebration Book. Waverly, IA: G & R Publishing, 2003.

Butler County Cemetery Records, vol. II. N.p.: Butler County Historical Society, 1987.

Butler County Centennial Fair Book. Waterloo, IA: Morris Publishing, 1956.

Butler County Courthouse Records. Allison, Iowa.

Butler County Genealogy Website. http://www.iagenweb.org/butler.

Butler County, Iowa Census. http://www.censusfinder.com/iowa2.htm.

Butler County Plat Book. N.p.: 1965.

Centennial of St. John's Evangelical Lutheran Church, Vilmar. Greene, Iowa. 1979.

Clarksville Star, April 1, 1875.

Dean, Valena. Interview with Fannie Albrecht. Valena grew up in the area of Norton's Corners and had pictures from that time period.

Diercks. Ruth P., ed. *A Type of Foxfire History from Butler County, Iowa*. Bristow, IA: PenDragon Press, 1976.

1883 Butler-Bremer County, Iowa History. Springfield, IL: Union Publishing Company, 1883.

Franken, Paul, and Fannie Franken Albrecht. Grew up in the Norton's Corners area and spearheaded getting reunions restarted and copied photos for the Shell Rock Historical Museum.

Friends of Butler Center website. http://www.uni.edu/biology/butlercenter/history.html.

From Here to There. Iowa Heritage: Program #6. Iowa Public Television, 1998.

Gates, Jim, and Linda Gates. Lowell Town historians. Researched Lowell and submitted information. Used with their permission.

Hart, Irving H. *History of Butler County, Iowa: A Record of Settlement, Organization, Progress and Achievement.* Chicago: S.J. Clarke Publishing Co., 1914.

Illustrated Historical Atlas of the State of Iowa Chicago: Andreas Atlas Co., 1875.

Iowa Ghost Towns Project. http://www.iowaghosttowns.com/butlercounty.htm.

Iowa State Gazetteer, 1865. Chicago.

Kaiser-Corson Funeral Homes. Supplied the names of current sextons.

Kothe, Ken. Transcribed the cemetery records and permitted use of them.

McLaughlin, John D., cont. *Bennezette Township History.*

Miller, Shirley. Coster historian. Submitted Coster information and used with her permission.

Mott, D.C. Annals of Iowa, vols. 17–18. Iowa State Historical Department, Des Moines, Iowa. *Abandoned Towns, Villages, and Post Offices of Iowa*, 1930–32.

Norton, James Byron. Research submitted to author and used with his permission. His family has lived in the Norton's Corners area since the 1850s.

Parkersburg Eclipse, February 1998.

Priepke, Rudolf. *Years Ago.* Clarksville, IA: Star Corp., 1978.

Randall, Linda Cassman. Butler Center pamphlet.

Sahr, Robert C. Inflation converter on the Internet. http://oregonstate.edu/cla/polisci/faculty-research/sahr/sahr.htm.

Savage, Tom. *A Dictionary of Iowa Place-Names.* Iowa City: University of Iowa Press, 2007.

Shell Rock News, August 24, 1924.

Shell Rock News, December 15, 1878.

Taylor, Isaac. *A History of the Origin of Place Names Associated with the Chicago and NorthWestern Railroad.* Chicago: 1908.

INDEX

ABOUT THE AUTHOR

Linda Betsinger McCann is a native Iowan who continues to live in Iowa by choice. Her ancestors settled in Iowa by the 1850s. Linda has been doing genealogy for about thirty years and recently traced a line to George Soule, who arrived on the *Mayflower*. She has been researching and writing the history of the area where she lives, and this is her tenth book. Linda has discovered that she most enjoys writing biographies and plans to do more of them. She dedicates all her books to her granddaughters because without them she probably would not have started writing. Linda hopes that her granddaughters will read the books and be proud to be Iowans, just as Linda is.

Visit us at
www.historypress.net